Dr. Evi Prokopi

The Success Playbook

The Success Playbook

Dr. Evi Prokopi

The Success Playbook

The 8 Habits of Happy & Successful People

Dr. Evi Prokopi

The Success Playbook

2020 All rights reserved.
All images by Evi Prokopi 2020.

Evi Prokopi
ISBN 9798664382464

Dr. Evi Prokopi

Acknowledgments

I would like to thank everyone who participated in my survey, Louisa Jordan, my editor, who had the patience to answer all my questions, and Dr. Andrea Ferrantelli who helped me with the Physics chapter.

Special thanks to my mother, Agrippina and my late father Spyros, who have supported all my decisions, and my brother, Thanos, who is the strongest and most successful person I know, even if he forgets it sometimes.

Table of Contents

2 Happiness and Success Research Results 27

3 Physics and Human Nature 45

Introduction

Most of us want to be able to achieve our goals and be happy. But it is not always easy. We do not know where to start. We were not born with a map to happiness. Or were we? We cannot help but wonder, and it is a good thing to wonder. How are we supposed to set goals and how can we achieve them? Will achieving our goals lead us to happiness or not? What is happiness? Is it subjective or is there an objective truth for everyone? This book lays the ground on answering these and more questions with wisdom and knowledge coming from research.

You may have heard of the law of attraction. It does not matter if you believe in it or not. What matters is your open mind. This book combines disciplines, such as psychology, ancient philosophy, and physics, and gives a scientific approach to the law of attraction. Science is actually in service of people's success and happiness—if people are willing to learn from it, and choose to learn who they really are.

As Albert Einstein said "A human being is a part of the whole called by us universe, a part limited in time and space. He experiences himself, his thoughts and feeling as something separated from the rest, a kind of optical delusion of his consciousness. This delusion is a kind of prison for us, restricting us to our personal desires and to affection for a few persons nearest to us. Our task must be to free ourselves from this prison by widening our circle of compassion to embrace all living creatures and the whole of nature in its beauty."

A Fairytale

In a kingdom far, far away, hundreds of years ago, people lived happily and the king was loved and respected by everyone. However, one day, a dragon started to attack the kingdom, burning crops and houses down. The villagers started to worry as they would soon run out of food and they were angry at the king.

The king asked his councilors for advice but they couldn't help him. The king then decided to go up the mountain where a wise guru lived and the guru told him that one of his options was to feed the children to the dragon so that he could calm him down.

The king didn't hear his other options. He ran to his kingdom and announced to everyone that children would need to be sacrificed so that the kingdom could be saved. He placed a big bucket in the central square and wrote down every child's name on a piece of paper. He put the pieces inside the bucket and every time the dragon would approach, he would take a piece and knew which child would need to be sacrificed. And as soon as the dragon had eaten a child, the dragon would not destroy anything and he would not set anything on fire.

However, the king's son, who would become the future king, believed that this tactic was unfair, and so he decided to secretly replace all the names of the children with his name so he would be the next one to be sacrificed. Next time the dragon approached the kingdom, the king pulled a piece out and read his heir's name. All of a sudden, the king started to rethink what he had been doing. So he ordered his knights to hunt down the dragon and kill him. And they lived happily ever after.

Dr. Evi Prokopi

1 Literature Review on Success and Happiness

1.1 Psychological Theories

In this chapter, we will explore ideas, concepts, theories, and paradigms taken from psychology, philosophy, and religion throughout history. Our goal is to get a grasp of what success and happiness are and how this has been perceived over the centuries by some of the brightest minds of the world.

The history of psychology dates back to the ancient Greeks. It is highly probable that the Babylonians and ancient Egyptians, among others, used concepts involving the mind, thought process, and behavior, but unfortunately all that valuable information was transmitted orally, and therefore lost. This is the reason why the ancient Greeks are used as a starting point in the history of psychology.

Psychology was a branch of philosophy until the 1870s. Psychology as a standalone field of study was introduced in 1879, when Wilhelm Wundt established the first psychological laboratory in Germany.

Once experimental psychology flourished, several types of applied psychology appeared. Mental testing appeared in the 1890s; while in Austria, Sigmund Freud, the father of psychoanalysis, developed his approach to the study of the mind that has been widely influential, even though criticized and rejected by several scientists in more recent years.

In the late 19th century, functionalism was introduced by the American psychologist Edward Thorndike, and the focus was on understanding why humans have developed the way they have, looking into the purpose of consciousness and behavior, their motives, and ideals.

The advent of the 20th century was marked by the formulation of behaviorism by John B. Watson, which was then studied even further by Burrhus Frederic Skinner. Behaviorism experts accept that the mind cannot be objectively studied, so they focus on studying behaviors because these can be measured. The idea is that behavior is acquired based on its consequences, which can be positive (as in reinforcements) and negative (as in punishments). Depending on the consequence, someone is more or less likely to repeat a specific behavior.

Around the same time, social psychology was developed by Lev Semyonovich Vygotsky who studied the awareness of circumstances surrounding individuals and how their behaviors are affected by social situations and cultures that surround them. He ultimately focused on how someone's experiences, influences, and culture shape why they think and act the way they do.

While the end of the 20th century was drawing near, cognitive science rose in popularity. Cognitive science, according to the American Psychological Association, is an interdisciplinary approach that studies the human mind and, specifically, mental processes such as attention, language use, memory, perception, problem solving, creativity, and thinking, using elements of psychology, linguistics, computer science, philosophy, behaviorism, and neurobiology. Cognitive science is used in developing artificial intelligence. Even though Ulric Neisser is considered the father of cognitive psychology, Jean Piaget's studies popularized it.

There have been a few schools of psychology, some more widely accepted than others. However, we are here to understand the common element amongst them when it comes to humans. The history of psychology is divided into four waves based on its schools, spanning from introspection and mental disease treatment, moving to psychoanalysis, and further to behaviorism and humanistic psychology, and finally concluding to positive psychology that shifts its focus from symptoms to acceptance, incorporating spiritualism and mindfulness.

Since we are focusing on success and happiness in this book, we are also focusing on specific psychological theories related to success, happiness, and self-actualization.

1.1.1 Hierarchy of Needs

Abraham Harold Maslow was an American psychologist and a psychology professor who emphasized the importance of focusing on the positive qualities in people, instead of their symptoms and issues. He was a leader of humanistic psychology and laid the foundation for the modern positive psychology movement. Maslow is best known for developing the hierarchy of needs, a motivational theory consisting of five stages, each one consisting of human needs. He introduced that we first need to cover our innate human needs in priority before we consider pursuing, or even care about, self-actualization.

He started working on his theory in 1943 and fully developed it in his 1954 book *Motivation and Personality*. Below, we see an illustration of Maslow's hierarchy of needs.[1]

According to this theory, each individual needs to cover their physiological, safety, love, and esteem needs in this order before they can reach self-actualization. His classification system reflects the global needs of individuals in a community as its base before rising to more acquired emotions. It also exhibits a motivation behind a person's behavior and how they move to the next level up.

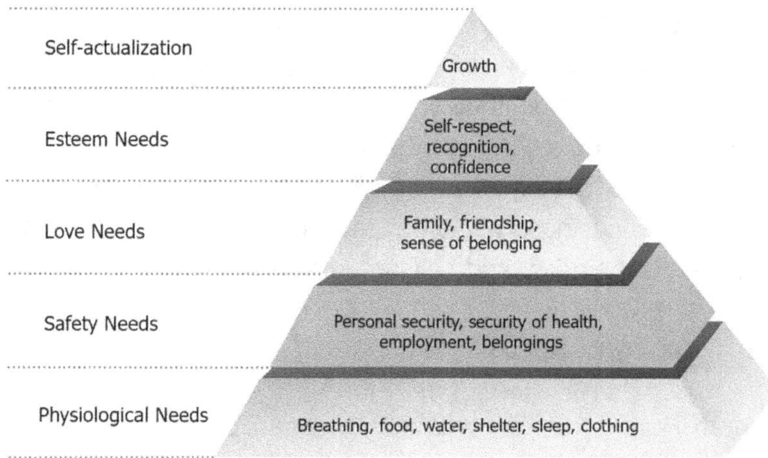

In other words, it makes perfect sense that one must first satisfy their needs for health, food, water, sleep, and hygiene before their motivation climbs up to the next level of safety of self and family, security of employment, and security of belongings. Once we have all these covered, we strive for love and a sense of belonging and we want friends and sexual intimacy in our lives. This level leads to the next one, consisting of self-esteem and confidence. We start to believe in ourselves and feel successful when we have secured our basic needs, employment, family, friends, and sexual intimacy. We become successful and that's also how we gain other people's respect. Once we feel confident, we try to achieve our self-actualization.

Self-actualization, according to Maslow, is the desire that leads to achieving one's potential, that is to becoming everything they are capable of becoming; a moral, creative human being who will solve problems, will support the community, and will lack prejudice. An important note by Maslow himself is that even though priorities do exist, it doesn't mean that one needs to cover a level completely before they try to rise to the next level. Partial satisfaction can also lead to the next level up.

The lower four levels are known as the "deficiency needs" and when they are not at least partially met, our personal development to self-actualization is obstructed because said needs only become bigger. If one is sick all the time, they crave their health more and more each day that passes by. On the other end, the fifth level consists of the "being needs." These needs are more like aspirations. They are related to one's desire for self-improvement and when they are at least partially met, this person is considered to achieve happiness.

Maslow's eye-opening theory sheds light on understanding the correlation between effort, motivation, and success when it comes to human behavior. Most of us wonder how we can achieve happiness, how we can become truly happy. Philosophers, psychologists, and coaches, such as Maslow, give us the answer. His hierarchy of needs is also known as the "pyramid of happiness."

When people realize that the meaning of life is to reach self-actualization, that's their a-ha moment and they begin to program their minds and organize their lives accordingly. Apparently, once we reach the level of self-actualization, we are also able to reach and maintain happiness.

Everyone can move up the hierarchy. However, progress is sometimes halted by a failure or a traumatic experience. There WILL be back and forths in the pyramid of happiness but we should never let a negative experience hinder our journey to happiness.

1.1.2 The Two-Factor Theory

The two-factor theory, also known as Herzberg's motivation-hygiene theory, was introduced by the psychologist Frederick Herzberg in 1959. It states that there are certain factors in the workplace that are related to job satisfaction and certain factors that are related to job dissatisfaction, all of which act independently of each other.

According to Herzberg's motivation-hygiene theory, people are not satisfied when they are simply paid a decent salary and work in a safe and pleasant workplace. As a matter of fact, they try to cover more high-level needs, such as sense of achievement, recognition, responsibility, and advancement. It is basically Maslow's hierarchy of needs with an additional dimension, a second factor. This second factor is about the lack of incentives, rewards, and advancement that leads to dissatisfaction at work. In other words, in order to improve productivity, we need to make the distinction between the two factors and both of them should be taken into account. Job satisfaction and job dissatisfaction are not opposites and an increase in satisfaction does not equal a decrease in dissatisfaction. Motivators such as achievement, personal growth, and responsibility increase employees' motivation and satisfaction while they contribute almost nothing to job dissatisfaction. On the other hand, hygiene factors, such as company practices, working conditions, and salary make almost no contribution to job satisfaction.

Hygiene factors, according to this theory, cause employees' dissatisfaction. Therefore, these factors must be removed in order to remove dissatisfaction. There are several ways that this can be done but some of the most important ways to decrease dissatisfaction would be to compensate employees' reasonably, to ensure their job security, and to create a nice environment in the workplace without micromanagement.

Once dissatisfaction factors are removed, our focus should be on ways (motivators) that increase satisfaction in the workplace. Employees are motivated when they are given new and challenging tasks, their efforts are recognized, and they can take up responsibilities. Research has shown that nowadays, people care more about the company culture and the development opportunities rather than the salary. Therefore, there are four possible cases:

1. The best workplace of the world. Great role, tasks, money, people, conditions consisting the BEST job for every individual.

High Hygiene	High Motivation	Highly Motivated Employees	Few Issues

2. A company working like a robot. People only complete necessary tasks, nothing extra. They work for the money.

High Hygiene	Low Motivation	Demotivated Employees	Few Issues

3. A company about to go bankrupt, about to fire people, thus not allowing room for personal development.

Low Hygiene	Low Motivation	Demotivated Employees	Many Issues

4. A company with great jobs and development opportunities, but low salaries and employees regularly work unpaid overtime.

Low Hygiene	High Motivation	Highly Motivated Employees	Many Issues

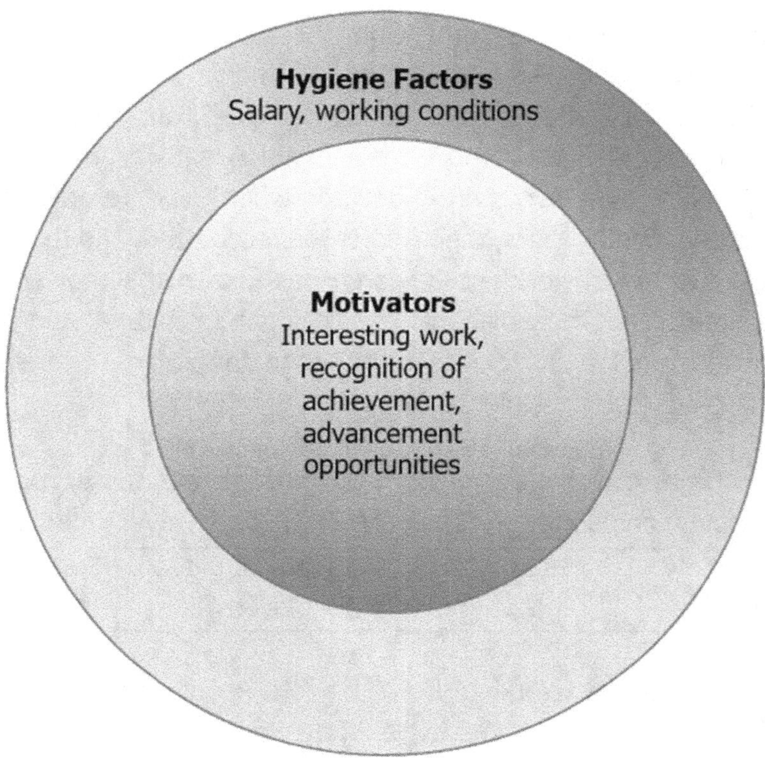

Considering that employees spend at least one third of their day at work, they should look for a job offering both high hygiene and high motivation factors. Apparently, the more motivated people are, the greater the chance is that they will reach self-actualization and this means that they are able to reach happiness.

1.1.3 Theory X and Theory Y

Theory X and Theory Y were introduced by Douglas McGregor, social psychologist and management professor at the MIT Sloan School of Management, in 1960. He developed the theories in his book *The Human Side of Enterprise* and they were greatly influenced by Maslow's hierarchy of needs. The two theories suggest that there are two opposite models of employees' motivation and are based on two sets of assumptions. Theory X is about the heightened supervision, intimidation, punishments, and micromanagement, while Theory Y highlights job satisfaction coming from self-actualization with minimum supervision.

Theory X
People dislike work
and avoid it if they can.

Theory Y
People are self-motivated
and want to work.

People must be forced to work.
People do not like to take responsibility.
People only work for the money.

People can work with minimal supervision.
People want to take on responsibilities.
People work to reach their potential.

Theory X suggests that an average employee does not like work or responsibilities and tries to avoid them whenever possible. They do not have any ambitions, and they only care about their salary. Therefore, they should be forced or warned with punishment in order to work. Their tasks and how these should be executed must be explained in full detail, and they should be closely supervised by their managers in order to achieve the company's objectives.

Managers adopting Theory X are authoritarian leaders who are results- and deadline-driven, intolerant, distant, arrogant, and trigger-happy. They sometimes bully their employees, they do not care about their team, and they are one-way communicators, that is they never listen to others. They usually think that their employees are lazy and less intelligent than them, so they take criticism badly and they are usually emotionally unstable. Consequently, they use rewards and punishments as motivation.

Theory Y, on the other hand, suggests that employees enjoy working and are self-motivated so they can reach company's objectives with minimal supervision, rewards, and punishments. As long as they find their job rewarding, they will be loyal to the company and they will want to take up more responsibilities.

Managers adopting Theory Y are democratic leaders who think that their employees are skilled, intelligent, and creative problem-solvers. They believe their team is valuable and they take care of it and protect it. Therefore, they create a friendly environment in the workplace and a sense of unity where they encourage every individual and help them improve, develop, and finally become a better version of themselves.

Sometimes, a leader needs to try both theories in order to understand which one works best with the people they manage in a specific workplace and under specific conditions. They also need to realize that their leadership style will affect their employees' motivation, efficiency, and productivity. Theory X may be implemented in an industrial environment because high productivity is required. Theory Y may be implemented in more sophisticated environments where critical thinking is required and employees are expected to innovate and act on their own.

To summarize, Theory X suggests a pessimistic view of employees' behavior at work where employees prioritize their physiological and safety needs, while Theory Y suggests an optimistic view where employees prioritize their esteem and social needs and then their self-actualization needs. At the end of the day, motivation depends on the individual's needs and how they prioritize them in order to achieve happiness.

1.1.4 The Two-Factor Theory of Emotion

The two-factor theory of emotion states that emotion is the result of two factors: physiological arousal and cognition.[2] The 1962 theory was created by Stanley Schachter, a social psychologist, and Jerome Singer, the founding chair of the Medical and Clinical Psychology Department at Uniformed Services University.

According to this theory, when an emotion is felt, a physiological arousal such as a fast heartbeat, sweating, shaking, shivering, or butterflies in the stomach occur and the individual uses the surrounding environment to search for the cause of this physiological arousal. For example, consider most people's reaction when they see a huge snake. They get a physiological response, such as shaking or an increased heartbeat, which internally shouts "feel fear." Respectively, when people celebrate New Year's Eve with loved ones, they may experience warmth, which in turn may be interpreted as happiness.

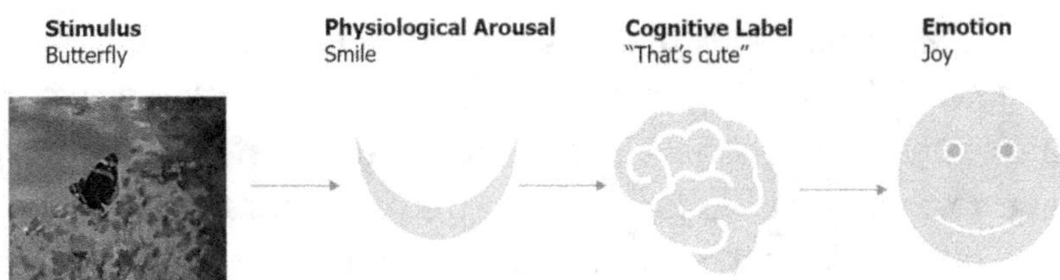

This theory focuses on the distinction between involuntary physiological arousals and the voluntary process of thinking and knowing and it comes down to the specific circumstances of every situation. The cognition, however, comes down to each individual's prior experiences and the entire process is completed within seconds without consciously thinking about how we should feel.

1.1.5 Attribution Theory

In 1958, the psychologist Fritz Heider talked about attribution theory in his book *The Psychology of Interpersonal Relations*, which explains the process used by individuals in order to interpret events and how these are tied to the way they think and act, in other words why people do what they do. He suggests that a certain behavior is determined by either internal attribution, where the individual feels responsible, in control, and chooses to behave a certain way due to their abilities or feelings, or external attribution, where the individual has no choice or control due to circumstances. For example, someone buys a computer and takes it home. When they turn it on, they only see a black screen and nothing is loading. If they believe this is happening because they don't know about computers, then this is an internal attribution. If they believe this is happening because the computer is broken, then this is an external attribution.

Research has shown that we are sometimes biased in our judgment of what or who is responsible for a situation as we try to maintain our confidence and positive image of ourselves. We tend to think that we fail due to external factors and we don't always assume responsibility. On the other hand, we tend to think that we succeed due to internal factors. If we are not looking at our failures objectively, our motivation and performance may be undermined because we will keep blaming external factors instead of assuming responsibility and becoming better.

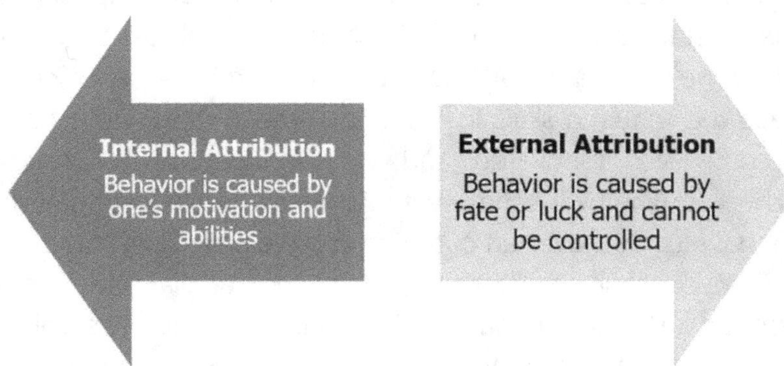

Attribution theory was further advanced by the social psychologist Bernard Weiner who talked about motivation and high achievers' traits. High achievers go after success because they believe it is a combination of skills and effort.

1.1.5.1 Attributional Retraining

According to the attribution theory, our behavior is determined by internal and external causal factors. What if we retrain our thinking regarding these attributions? If we intervene with attributional retraining, motivation will be enhanced and dysfunctional thinking will be eliminated. With this retraining, people adopt more positive perceptions of their skills and abilities that increase motivation. Attributional retraining techniques are used to restructure an individual's explanations about personal failure so that they are perceived with positive cognition.

Studies have shown that whenever attributional retraining has been implemented, performance was ameliorated because individuals' thoughts and beliefs along with unhelpful explanations affecting motivations and performance outcomes were replaced by positive and helpful thoughts and explanations that sustained motivation. This shouldn't come as a surprise. When we believe we CANNOT do something because we do not have the required skills in order to succeed, then we instantly become less motivated and we do not pursue success. However, when we believe we CAN do something, we feel that we have control over an outcome and we strive and thrive.

The concept of retraining should be familiar. We are all familiar with resocialization during imprisonment or psychiatric hospitalization. Resocialization is the process through which people are reprogrammed in order to follow values and rules, generally accepted by society and communities. Prisons and psychiatric hospitals use resocialization techniques so that when inmates and patients are released, they can be adapted to society and its norms.

We will come back to mind retraining later in this book, because it is truly the essence of success. Our attitude is by a large percentage what leads us to success or failure, thus we need to retrain our mind in order to achieve success and happiness, as long as this is what we want.

1.2 Lessons Learned from Ancient Greek Philosophy

Philosophy was used to understand the world in a nonreligious way and it dealt with a variety of subjects, such as astronomy, mathematics, and politics, among others. Greek philosophy has influenced Western culture and is a wealth of knowledge. In this section, we focus on some of the ancient wisdom about happiness and success.

1.2.1 Plato

Plato was an ancient Greek philosopher, Socrates' student, and teacher of Aristotle. He introduced the Theory of Soul, suggesting that the psyche is the essence of a person, where all knowledge is stored, and is what determines a person's behavior.

The soul consists of three ruling parts: reason, anger, and desire. Reason seeks for the truth. It feeds with knowledge and wants to distinguish between what is real, unreal, true, and false. Anger is what makes us angry but it loosely includes courage. In a fair soul, anger and reason work together so the individual is a good person. In an unfair soul, anger ignores reason and makes demands. Desire is about love, hunger, and thirst and it generally opposes reason because desire is an instinct.

The healthy mind balances all three parts, according to Plato. People who have one of these traits more dominant, compared to the other two, are good on certain things. For example, city leaders should have reason as their dominant trait while salesmen would thrive if they had desire as their dominant trait, and good soldiers have anger as their dominant trait.

Plato once said that "Courage is knowing what not to fear" and "Follow your dream as long as you live, do not lessen the time of following desire, for wasting time is an abomination of the spirit." If we follow Plato's advice, as long as we live we should try to chase our dreams with courage until we become happy.

1.2.2 Socrates

Socrates, the founder of Western philosophy, believed that we need to know ourselves in order to achieve happiness. Our choices are motivated by the pursuit of happiness but happiness is achieved only when the right choices are made. Right choices, therefore, are made by those who truly know themselves.

According to Socrates, we are happy if we can truly focus on and appreciate what we have instead of striving to get more and more. He said "The secret of happiness, you see, is not found in seeking more, but in developing the capacity to enjoy less."

Socrates strongly believed that nobody can force their views and beliefs on other people in order to bring a lasting change. Individuals need to think and accept theories and beliefs on their own volition and pace. Therefore, even if we want to help someone realize they need to address a matter, we can only try to help them think in a different direction, then wait for them until they realize there is something wrong on their own and let them choose if they want to do something about it.

1.2.3 Epictetus

Epictetus taught philosophy as a way of life and strongly believed that happiness is achieved from within. He said "He is a wise man who does not grieve for the things which he has not, but rejoices for those which he has" and that "There is only one way to happiness and that is to cease worrying about things which are beyond the power of our will." When we focus on what we have, we realize how much we truly have. Sometimes, we take things like drinking clean water, having a hot shower, breathing with an unblocked nose, and sleeping on a mattress for granted.

Epictetus pointed out that we often worry about future situations that may never come and we rarely worry about real problems. We stress over things that may never happen. We worry about things that lie outside our control. We only need to focus on what WE can do in the present and how we can improve ourselves starting now.

1.2.4 Aristotle

Aristotle who discussed physics, metaphysics, poetry, theater, rhetoric, and politics, among other things, strongly believed that "Happiness is the meaning and the purpose of life, the whole aim and end of human existence and it depends upon ourselves" and that "Braver [is the one] who overcomes his desires than him who conquers his enemies, for the hardest victory is over the self."

To correlate to what we have discussed so far, and understand how his theories inspired Epictetus, Aristotle was the first to say that negative thoughts may cross people's minds but what distinguishes wise men from the rest is the fact that the wise people will not accept these negative thoughts as their truth. We need to distinguish between thoughts that do us good from those that do us harm. When we focus on misery, failure, and pain, this is what prevails and we need to eliminate this source of unhappiness. We need to focus on the bright side, as there is always a bright side.

1.2.5 Plotinus

Plotinus realized that "True satisfaction is only for what has its plentitude in its own being; where craving is due to an inborn deficiency, there may be satisfaction at some given moment but it does not last." Even if we succeed, even if we reach our goals, it seems that the good feelings do not last and we need to do something about it. Plotinus suggested to:

> "Withdraw into yourself and look. And if you do not find yourself beautiful yet, act as does the creator of a statue that is to be made beautiful: he cuts away here, he smoothes there, he makes this line lighter, this other purer, until a lovely face has grown upon his work. So do you also: cut away all that is excessive, straighten all that is crooked, bring light to all that is overcast, labor to make all one glow of beauty and never cease chiseling your statue, until there shall shine out on you from it the godlike splendor of virtue, until you shall see the perfect goodness surely established in the stainless shrine."

No matter how far we have gone, we always need to introspect and create a better version of ourselves.

1.3 Traditional Chinese Religion Views

Traditional Chinese religion or Chinese folk religion suggests that reality can be influenced by humans as well as spirits and gods. It is heavily influenced by Confucianism, Taoism, and Buddhism in combination with local folk beliefs and practices from Shamanism. One could say that this religion is more like a philosophy than a religion and one could follow beliefs without adhering to their gods. It is noteworthy that family is highly regarded in Chinese folk religion and it is considered to be the moral basis of society.

In this section, we will dwell in the wisdom shared by this religion, which has a lot in common with ancient Greek philosophy. We will focus on Buddha, Confucius, and Lao Tzu.

1.3.1 Buddha

Buddha was a philosopher, spiritual teacher, and religious leader who lived in ancient India, and was the founder of Buddhism. Buddha realized that we are able to reach success and happiness if we think positively. He said "All that we are is a result of what we have thought." We just have to take small steps toward our goals, focus on each step, and go for it. Of course, we need to work hard because success comes to those who try. Once you set your mind to being successful, keep thinking positively and start working hard for what you want.

Buddhism acknowledges that failure is part of life and that's why the *Dhammapada*, the collection of Buddha's sayings, highlights "Do not dwell in the past, do not dream of the future, concentrate the mind on the present moment." We should never focus on negative experiences from the past and we should never worry about the future. We should only focus on the present because we learn a lot more during hard work than when we actually reach our goal, provided that we reflect on our work, on what went well, and what went wrong so that we understand why we made mistakes and learn how to avoid making the same mistakes in the future.

When we think positively, we allow some space to appreciate what we have. Buddha said "Health is the greatest gift, contentment the greatest wealth, faithfulness the best relationship." How many times do we take a minute to appreciate that we are alive and we can feel the sun's warm rays surrounding us on a summer day? Thich Nhat Hanh, a

Vietnamese monk who founded the Plum Village Tradition, a school of Buddhism, once said "When we are tired and feel discouraged by life's daily struggles, we may not notice these miracles, but they are always there."[3]

1.3.2 Confucius

Confucius was a Chinese philosopher and politician. His philosophy, also known as Confucianism, highlighted morality, justice, kindness, and sincerity. Similar to Buddha's attitude, he believed in hard work and embraced failure.

> "Success depends upon previous preparation, and without such preparation there is sure to be failure. Our greatest glory is not in never falling, but in rising every time we fall. The will to win, the desire to succeed, the urge to reach your full potential...these are the keys that will unlock the door to personal excellence."

He believed that people make mistakes and should learn from them. That's why he said "Study the past if you would define the future." When we understand the consequences of our mistakes, we can try again while we avoid making the same mistakes and thus approach our goals. Just like Buddha, he believed that it's okay to go slowly as long as you do not stop, because he emphasized on the importance of small steps at a time.

Regarding work, Confucius thought that if we do a job that we enjoy then we will give our passion and energy and it will feel as if we are not actually working. He said that "Choose a job you love, and you will never have to work a day in your life."

Finally, just like Buddha and the ancient Greeks, he believed that life is very simple, but we tend to make it complicated. Things are rather simple if we focus on our present time and appreciate all that is given to us in abundance.

1.3.3 Lao Tzu

Laozi, also known as Lao Tzu, was an ancient Chinese philosopher, the author of the *Tao Te Ching* and the founder of Taoism.

Similarly to Buddha and Confucius, Laozi also believed in small steps. That's why he said "A journey of a thousand miles begins with a single step." He appreciated health and he believed it was the greatest possession and was a firm believer of living in the moment and appreciating all one has as that is the way to reach happiness.

> "If you are depressed, you are living in the past. If you are anxious, you are living in the future. if you are at peace, you are living in the present. Be content with what you have, rejoice in the way things are. When you realize there is nothing lacking, the whole world belongs to you."

Finally, he strongly believed in how positive or negative thinking alters our reality, helps us, or obstructs us in our journey.

> "Watch your thoughts, they become your words. Watch your words, they become your actions. Watch your actions, they become your habits. Watch your habits, they become your character. Watch your character, it becomes your destiny. Be careful what you water your dreams with.

Water them with worry and fear and you will produce weeds that choke the life from your dream. Water them with optimism and solutions and you will cultivate success. Always be on the lookout for ways to turn a problem into an opportunity for success. Always be on the lookout for ways to nurture your dream."

1.4 The Law of Attraction

You may have heard of the Law of Attraction but do you know much about it? Do you know about its origins? The Law of Attraction is about the ability to attract whatever we are focusing on. It suggests that when one uses the power of the mind, they can turn their thoughts into reality. You may have already found the similarities in what you read on the previous pages about ancient Greek philosophy and traditional Chinese religion and you may have noticed that there aren't many differences between those and the Law of Attraction. We already know that our thoughts make us what we are and with hard work and positive thinking we can achieve our goals.

In the 19th century, the New Thought movement developed in the United States. It has been rumored that this movement was influenced by the unpublished writings of Phineas Quimby, an American mentalist and mesmerist. Supporters of the movement believe in positive thinking, the law of attraction, healing, creative visualization, and personal power.

Helena Blavatsky was a Russian occultist and philosopher and the first one to use the term "the Law of Attraction" in 1877.[4] Blavatsky believed that humans are able to shape reality and that our thoughts about ourselves define us. She also thought that a failure may be an undercover success as she said "Do not be afraid of your difficulties. Do not wish you could be in other circumstances than you are. For when you have made the best of an adversity, it becomes the stepping stone to a splendid opportunity."

Several authors have adopted and used the term since then, and some of them have also created spin offs. In 1910, Wallace Wattles, a New Thought author, wrote *The Science of Getting Rich* and highlighted that individuals should develop their own manifestations instead of waiting for experts to teach them. He offered techniques that anyone could use and adapt as per their own goals, and he encouraged creative visualization, which remains a significant practice of the Law of Attraction. Just like his predecessors, he believed in hard work and acceptance of failure and claimed that one should:

> "Do all the work you can do, every day, and do each piece of work in a perfectly successful manner; put the power of success, and the purpose to get rich, into everything that you do. Go on in the certain way, and if you do not receive that thing, you will receive something so much better that you will see that the seeming failure was really a great success."

He also believed that "By thought, the thing you want is brought to you; by action you receive it."[5]

Nowadays, more and more people become familiar with the Law of Attraction, partly because of Rhonda Bryne's book (and later movie) *The Secret* that presents the views of a wide range of Law of Attraction practitioners. It emphasizes the importance of setting goals appropriately and learning new ways of thinking in order to get what you want.

1.5 Conclusion

We all want to be happy. But what is happiness? Aristotle suggested that happiness is in achieving all the goods, such as health, wealth, knowledge, love, and friends in the course of a lifetime. He believed that all these lead to the perfection of human nature. Positive psychology and recent research have shown that happiness is more of a state of mind than something happening to us so it suggests that if we stop blaming external factors for our unhappiness, we will find the power to change our thoughts and ultimately make ourselves happy.

In 2010, Morten Kringelbach, professor of neuroscience, and Kent Berridge, professor of psychology and neuroscience, conducted research about the Neuroscience of Happiness and Pleasure.[6] Based on their research, and given the fact that humans are social beings, data indicated that one of the most important factors for happiness is social relationships with other people. After all, the Dalai Lama once said "My religion is very simple. My religion is kindness" and Laozi said that "Being deeply loved by someone gives you strength, while loving someone deeply gives you courage." Indeed, it seems that being kind and giving love are essential parts of peace and happiness.

In 2009, Kringelbach said that one way to conceive happiness is as "liking" without "wanting."[7] That is, a state of pleasure without disruptive desires, a state of contentment. Does this sound familiar? Yes, it does sound familiar as you will find it paraphrased in the previous pages.

Therefore, it seems that when we set clear goals, we take a step at a time, we think positively, we focus on our goals, and work hard for them. Even if we fail and fall, we need to have a little faith, get up, and keep trying until we succeed in everything. Having faith has nothing to do with religious faith.

It means to believe that you can fight and win. It means to keep rising no matter how many times you stumble and fall.

1.6 Assignment for Reflection

Write down which quotes and theories resonate with you and you are setting in your mind from now on. Moreover, write down all the things and people that matter to you at the moment and prioritize them. Add a note about your feelings. Are you happy with your prioritization?

2 Happiness and Success Research Results

2.1 Background Information

In 2020, I decided to conduct a study on success and happiness to understand how these are perceived in the Western world. Thanks to my LinkedIn network, and of course friends and family, several hundreds of people were kind enough to answer the survey, mainly from Austria, Germany, Greece, Italy, Poland, Spain, the UK, and the USA. The survey was completely anonymous and consisted of 24 questions.

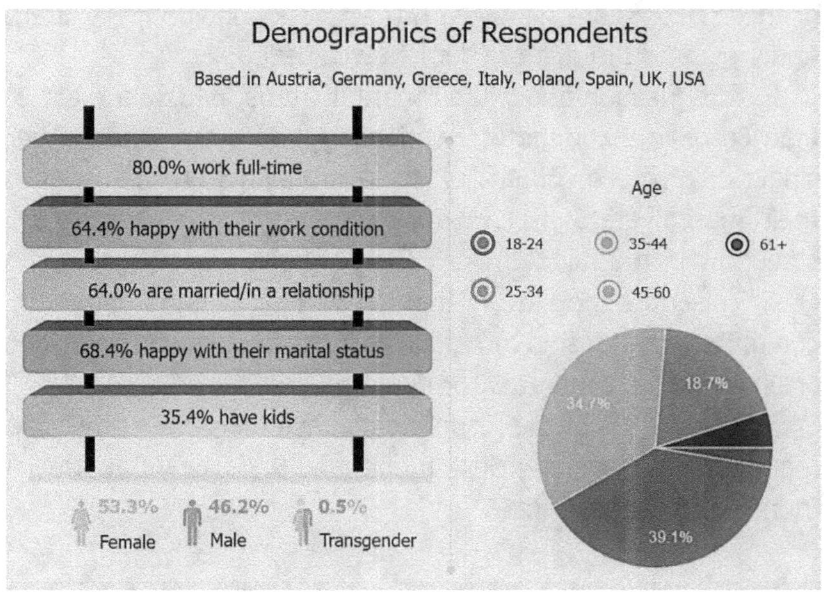

In general, I received very positive feedback about the questions that were heavily influenced by the psychological theories analyzed in the previous pages, and a lot of people told me something along the lines of "thank you for reminding me how much I have." It seems that when someone reminds people what they already have, they remember to appreciate them and feel happier, and of course I am happy for helping them achieve this!

The results revealed some amazing insights. Considering demographics, 53.3% of the respondents are men, 46.2% women, and 0.5% transgender. Regarding their age, 2.7% are between 18–24, 39.1% are between 25–34, 34.7% are between 35–44, 18.7% are between 45–60, and 4.8% are over 60 years old.

Among the respondents, 80.0% work full-time, 10.2% work part-time, 3.1% are retired, and 6.7% are unemployed; 64.4% of these people are happy with their work condition, 9.4% are unhappy, and the rest are somehow satisfied.

In the question about their marital status, 64.0% are either married or in a committed relationship and the rest are either single or divorced; 68.4% of the respondents are happy with their marital status, 11.9% are unhappy, and the rest are somehow in the middle. Only 35.4% of the respondents have kids. This does not mean that all who are married or in a committed relationship have kids as some people who have kids are now single, separated, or divorced.

Finally, 63.6% of the respondents have more than one close friend, 26.7% have one close friend, and 9.7% only have social friends and acquaintances.

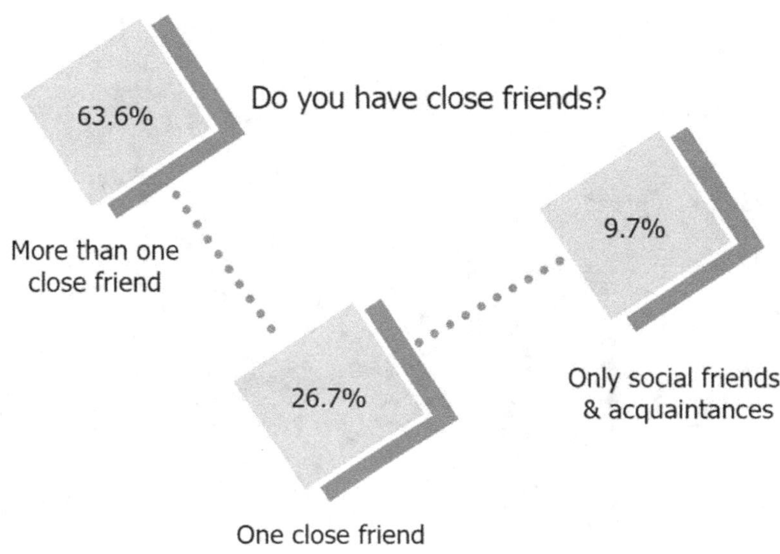

2.2 What People Consider as Success

The majority of respondents (68.9%) think that one has to try in order to be successful, and 27.6% of them think that it may be a combination of hard work and luck.

Regarding lifetime success, 97.8% believe that they have been successful at least once in their life with more than half of them (70.3%) having been successful within the last year from the time of answering the survey.

When they answered in which domains they have been successful at least once in their lifetime, the answers were varied but the staggering majority (75.1%) had been successful at work, 65.3% at education, obtaining a diploma or a certification, and 64.4% had been successful physically and mentally.

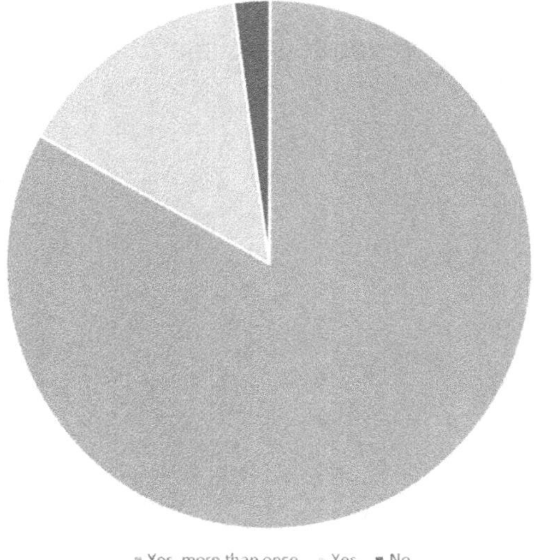

The majority ultimately covered their esteem needs with 66.2% being successful in friendships and having at least one good friend and 60.8% having a loving partner whom they love back; however, from those married and in a committed relationship, 5.6% did not feel like this. Regarding family, 49.8% get along well with their parents and they are close to each other and 28.0% get along well with their kids and are close to each other. It is noteworthy that this leaves 21.2% of the parents who responded without good relationships with their kids.

Finally, 48.4% claim they have as much money as they need to live a nice life and provide for those they care about. Some people said that they are successful because they can travel while some others focused on the fact that they are surrounded by people who treat them with respect. A couple of people mentioned that they started their own business and one them specifically said "I battled myself and won."

Some of the most fascinating answers, in my opinion, were given to the question "Which of the following makes someone successful in your opinion?" This question gave a long list of answers to select, as many as the respondents wanted to, and also gave the option to add additional answers, if the respondents wished to do so.

Interestingly, 70.2% of the respondents agreed that success is to maintain one's health. Considering that this answer was just before the outbreak of COVID-19, I find it amazing and self-conscious. However, it is remarkable that the rest (28.2%) do not consider being healthy as a success. It leads me to wonder whether these people can truly appreciate the importance of good physical and mental health. I am also wondering whether their answers would have been any different if they had answered during the pandemic.

Which of the following makes someone successful in your opinion?

Maslow might have been disappointed if he had read that only 56.4% consider success as having enough food and drinking water and 56.0% consider success as having a safe shelter to sleep and use for hygiene purposes. These are followed with 48.0% for the security of employment and 32.9% for the security of property. It should be mentioned that 37.3% of the people answered that someone is successful when they have zero debt.

What is interesting is that only 24.0% consider someone owning a house as successful and only 17.0% consider someone owning a car. Even if it seems that material goods are not necessarily what people consider as a proof of success, only 11.6% of the respondents marked "be a business owner even though they don't earn a lot of money," in contrast with 29.3% who marked "be a business owner earning a lot of money," so money does change some people's perception.

On the other hand, most of the traits associated with a successful person seem to be related with love, esteem, and self-actualization, in other words, the higher levels of Maslow's pyramid: 68.4% of the respondents believe that someone is successful when they are feeling loved by one's family and 62.7% when they are feeling loved by one's partner; 54.2% find someone successful when they have a sense of belonging with friends and 64.0% when one feels confident; less than half of the people who answered (46.7%) believe that achieving at least one goal makes someone successful, which is a paradox, considering that the majority of them felt they had been successful over the previous year because they achieved a goal!; 67.6% think that when someone feels respected by others and is treated fairly, they are successful but only 57.8% think the other way around, that is respecting others and being fair to them; and over half of the respondents (56.9%) think that feeling free to be creative and feeling free to be spontaneous (39.5%) are signs of success.

Considering the fact that divorce rates fluctuate between 50% and 60% in Western countries, 46.7% consider someone successful if they are happily married and 46.2% if someone has at least one kid in a happy marriage. It is impressive that 10.7% consider someone having kids as successful even if this person is in an unhappy marriage, divorced, or separated. It is worth mentioning that someone specifically wrote that what makes someone successful, among other things, is "having happy kids regardless of the couple's relationship."

A few people brought up that someone is considered successful if they enjoy their work, if they can travel the world, if they have a sense of purpose and fulfilment, or if they can feel happiness. A couple of people mentioned that someone successful has a happy and healthy pet and feels loved regardless of relationships and whether they have a family. Quoting a respondent: "Success is in the eye of the person." Ultimately, success should be subjective.

Moving on with the research, the next question was about the feelings of the respondents when they achieved success. It is not surprising that 73.7% felt happy or satisfied and 22.7% felt confident. It is impressive that a few people (1.7%) said they felt empty, tired, or self-critical.

2.3 What People Consider as Happiness

Inspired by Maslow's pyramid of happiness, my first question was about the needs that the respondents have satisfied: 96.4% of the respondents can buy food and have access to drinking water and 92.9% are in good health in general; 82.2% own or rent their own house; 91.6% can pay their monthly bills and medical bills; the vast majority (over 80%) can afford going out once a week, buy presents for their loved ones, and travel at least once a year; 76.9% can afford their hobbies; and 65.8% can even save money.

Based on these answers and considering Maslow's pyramid, people should report a high percentage of happiness. Let's see what they really reported.

When people were asked what they felt when they were successful, most of them said that they felt either happy or

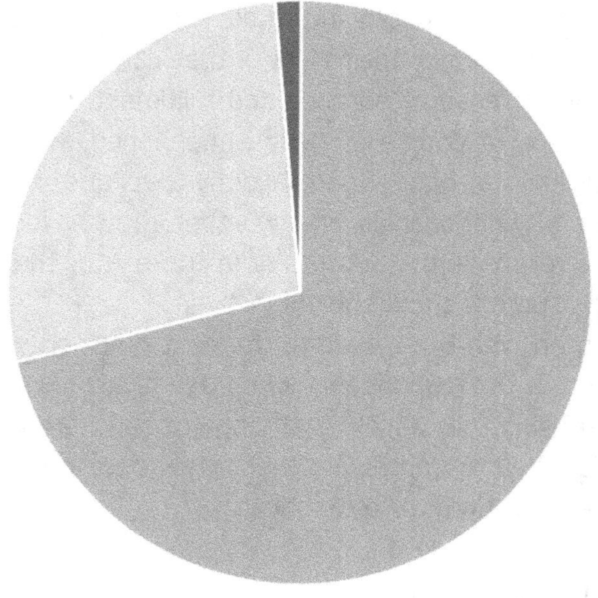

confident. Digging deeper and focusing on whether they feel happy when they are successful, 97.3% answered positively; however, 27.1% of those who answered positively made a note about their happiness lasting only a few days.

My next question asked the respondents to specify how happy they've felt over the past 12 months, on a scale from 1 to 10. Considering that 1–4 is in the low end, 5–7 in the middle, and 8–10 in the high end, only 49.8% are in the high end. On the bright side, only 14.2% are in the lower end and the rest (36.0%) are somewhere in the middle.

I then asked the respondents to prioritize certain aspects in their life. The aspects are family, work, sex, money, friends, free time for themselves, hobbies, love, and traveling. Answers were impressively varied. As their first priority, 26.2% of the respondents set family, while love is the first priority for 19.1% and free time for myself for 12.9% of them. When it comes to the second priority, 16.4% said it is their work, 12.3% their hobbies, and 12.0% replied it is their friends with another 12.0% placing sex in the second priority. Regarding their third priority, 15.4% said it is traveling, 14.6% money, and 13.0% sex. I found it rather interesting that as their last priority, that is number nine, 18.6% set their family, 18.2% set love, and 10.4% their hobbies.

I followed up wondering whether the respondents are happy with the priorities in their lives and the majority (76.9%) are indeed happy. Only 11.1% are unhappy and the rest (12.0%) find their prioritization mainly okay.

What was really surprising was the answers I received in the following question, asking "If you don't feel happy over the last 12 months, is it because you..." and then there was a list of things they could select and a blank option for people to write what they wanted and even though in the previous questions almost half of the respondents said they are happy, only 7.7% of the respondents said they are happy here.

Very low percentages were not happy because they were unable to meet their basic needs. Specifically, only 2.2% cannot buy food, 4.4% cannot afford a place to live, and a slightly higher percentage of 9.3% cannot pay their monthly bills; 0.9% stated that they are not happy because they do not have a kid and 1.4% of people said they are unhappy when they argue with their kids. I found it rather interesting that a respondent stated that they are not happy because of "fear of the future."

The majority of the respondents, that is 33.8%, are not happy with their job and this is completely aligned with 64.6% of the people who said in a previous question that they are happy with their work condition; and 32.0% are not happy because they do not have free time, 27.6% because they cannot save money, and 24.9% because of their relationship or marriage. Remember that 68.5% of the respondents previously answered they are happy with their marital status, so this was expected.

Another interesting insight is that only 13.3% answered they are not happy because they have been sick more than three times over the last 12 months. This is because 92.9% are in good health in general. I am wondering whether this was an opportunity to remind themselves they are not happy?

Naturally, my next question explored what makes people happy. It was an open question so I received many different answers and a few people wrote more than one thing that makes them happy. There were simple things, such as music, being close to nature, reading, dancing, food and wine, having free time, and doing nothing at times. Some people said it is actually life itself that makes them happy while others, more cynical, said it is money. Furthermore, eight people said it is their dog(s) that makes them happy and one person said it is their cat. What is impressive but sad is that a few people could not answer the question and said that they are still looking for what makes them happy.

However, the large majority, 53.3%, agreed that love, either by partners, kids, siblings, or other relatives, is what makes them happy; 20.2% said that their friends make them happy and 3.8% are happy when they feel valued and appreciated—it seems that a big part of happiness is made up by our interpersonal relations; 12.5% find happiness in their job and 3.0% when they achieve their goals and success; only 12.0% said that good health makes them happy while 11.5% talked about peace, calmness, balance, and a life of purpose; and finally, 11.0% of the respondents are happy when they have the freedom to choose and be creative and 6.7% are happy when they can travel and explore new places and experiences.

I loved reading the following particular comment: "beauty is in the eye of the beholder and happiness can be found and created in everything."

2.4 Other Insights

One of my closing questions dealt with luck. I wondered how lucky the respondents felt over the course of their lifetime from 1 to 10. With such positivity, I expected to see a high score. I was not wrong.

Considering that 1–4 is in the low end, 5–7 in the middle, and 8–10 in the high end, only 4.9% felt unlucky and a remarkable 63.5% felt lucky. The rest (31.6%) are in the middle but even then, they are mostly in the higher end of the middle.

Finally, I asked whether anyone wanted to add any comments and I loved what I read so I decided to share some of the best ones!

"The most precious thing is health! For all the other things you have to try hard to get what you deserve!" I cannot stress this enough. Health is the utmost good one can have. Unfortunately, many people only think about it and appreciate it when they are ill or when they see a loved one suffering.

> "I'm trying to feel happy and content in the moment and immersed in it rather than worrying about the future or ruminating on the past, or comparing myself to people with a lot of socially valuable achievements—being happy depends on what I put value on. I'm trying to put value on the moment and be compassionate with myself rather than put value on what society deems makes a successful person."

This person not only realizes the importance of living in the present but they also understand that one should only care about their personal goals and what matters to them and not to anyone else.

"This questionnaire made me already realize (again) that everything that I need is already there. I just have to grab it and own it." Appreciating what we have is the key to happiness. So many wise people said it hundreds of years before me.

"Society conditions people that happiness comes from material objects, vanity, and a partner or family. Happiness should come from within." Again, we should stop wondering what others think. We should only focus on our life and how we can make the best out of it, without becoming a burden to anyone.

> "I see work environment as the most important factor in our day to day happiness, because it is where we must spend the majority of our time. Some people underestimate its importance in terms of overall happiness. When I changed jobs, I went from a 4 to 9 in terms of happiness!"

I am so happy for this person who not only realized what made them unhappy but, worked hard and achieved their goal to change jobs. Now they are happy and so deserve it!

I am sincerely touched by the following statement that, in my opinion, summarizes the happy person's perspective.

> "I moved countries in order to escape 'poverty' and lack of opportunities. I changed jobs when I was unhappy... Being happy is quite important to me and staying in a bad situation just because it's familiar does not work for me. I believe that to be happy you need to say no to the things that make you unhappy. When it comes to success I believe everyone needs to define it for themselves. Taking some obsolete societal definitions (like make a lot of money, buy a big house, get that fancy car) won't make people happy as these are not things that feed your soul. Celebrate every time you can be yourself and you are loved. That's success and happiness in one."

"Really, I don't feel just lucky right now. I feel utterly blessed. Being unemployed and struggling to find my way in a new career, I'm quite scared about what will happen to me and my son but I know I have the skills and patience to rebuild, and for that my gratitude has no end. Thanks for asking these questions." This is the successful person's attitude. Remember what we said about faith? A Greek proverb says "I'll fall ten times and I'll rise eleven times." That's what you should do in order to achieve success.

"Remember Pasteur. Chance favors the prepared mind." I was so thrilled to read this quote by Louis Pasteur. Pasteur was a microbiologist and chemist and invented the process of pasteurization, that is the process in which water, milk, and fruit juice are treated with mild heat to eliminate pathogens and extend shelf life. When you are ready to transform your life, luck will help you achieve your new, best version.

"Money will lead you towards happiness. We just need to control desires and fulfill needs." Another honest view. Money will always be necessary in our society. You can cover several needs with money, such as food, water, and housing. However, so many rich people are not happy because they do not know how to control desires and feel joy and contentment over simple things. There may be massive peer pressure but more often than not, it is not peer pressure that makes us do, want, look for something. It is our own internal pressure because we see other people doing, wanting, looking for something, and we have to learn how to distinguish this and fight it. We do not have to imitate others, or role models that do not offer us real happiness.

"Not entirely sure that this question set does track success in my opinion. Success is not happiness." Absolutely. This is exactly what the research showed. As we have already seen, 97.8% of the respondents believe that they have been successful at least once in their life with more than half of them (70.3%) having been successful within the last year from time of answering but only 49.8% are happy during the same timeframe. Success brings happiness but very often this is a state that will only last for a while.

"Time with family is the most precious commodity." I love my family so much that I could not agree more. However, I need to recognize that sometimes the family we come from may be dysfunctional and that is why we need to be careful when we create our own family so we do not repeat the mistakes our ancestors made.

"I would describe success less as acquiring things that successful people tend to have, and more as discovering what drives you and what purpose you want to have in the world, and finding fulfillment through being able to achieve that." As we briefly discussed above, we need to get rid of internal pressure.

"I am as much happy as much my mind allows me." Closing, I think this succinct comment concentrates an ultimate truth. Considering that the vast majority has their needs as well as most of their desires covered, they should be happy. If not, it is because they need to retrain their minds.

2.5 Success and Happiness in the Western World

How do people relate success to happiness in the Western world? Based on this research, success leads to momentarily happiness. Many people feel happy when they achieve a goal. However, as time goes by, people get used to the achievement and start pursuing another goal, or focus on unpleasant situations. This does not come as a surprise as it has been observed that we get used to both good and bad things in our lives.

When something bad and unexpected happens, we channel all our energy to the specific situation. We tend to forget other things that bug us. For example, if we become ill, we tend to forget that we are stressing over a promotion or a salary raise that is not coming. We focus on getting well and do not stress over other things that may seem trivial when we lie weak in bed. Once we get well, we recall that we really want to get this promotion or salary raise.

Even though almost half of the respondents said that they are currently happy, when they were given the opportunity to talk about what currently makes them unhappy, the percentage of happy people dropped dramatically, and only 7.7% of the respondents said they are happy. It seems that when you give someone the option to be happy, it is quite likely that they will focus on happy thoughts. Accordingly, when you give someone the option to be unhappy, they will focus on unhappy thoughts.

Success and happiness have more in common than we would expect. Both need hard work and they are both subjective. We often confuse what others consider success and happiness and we press ourselves to do things that do not offer us either. We buy expensive smartphones, cars, clothes, and so on, because our friend or a celebrity we admire uses the same, or because we perceive these people as successful and we want to look like them. However, keep in mind that the fact that someone owns something expensive does not mean they are happy. Therefore, you may not be happy either, no matter how much you charge your credit card.

2.6 Do People Need to Be Happy to Be Successful?

Success brings moments of happiness but it is not what makes people remain happy forever. Happiness, on the other hand, is a state of mind, and happy people seem to achieve success more easily. It seems that happy people think positive and are not afraid of hard work because they know and they have faith that whatever they set their mind to, they can achieve it, even if they fail before they succeed.

2.7 Conclusion

The findings of the survey are more than interesting. They are eye-opening. The moral of this survey, the way I see it, is that once we learn how to not be affected by unfulfilled desires, we enjoy a much calmer and pleasant life compared to the people who keep chasing the latest smartphone model, car, designer couture, villa, and other goods, especially when they cannot afford them. As someone pointed out, battling ourselves is the essence of personal development. We race against ourselves more often than we realize and we need to focus on the reward of this race. That should be our real happiness; what will ultimately make **us** happy and not what we think makes others happy.

I would like to stress once again the importance of health. We all sometimes take it for granted and we forget how important it is to be physically and mentally healthy. Being unhealthy, however, is not a reason to give up on your dreams. Many famous people were successful while they were sick, such as Freddy Mercury who had AIDS when he recorded "Don't stop me now," Marie Curie who suffered from aplastic anemia because of exposure to radiation, and Edgar Allan Poe who was battling with depression. Sometimes, poor health is a motivation to be more productive but we need to feel grateful for our good health and we should remember that we can always achieve greatness.

2.8 Assignment for Reflection

Write down a goal you wish to achieve in the next three months, and keep a journal of how much effort you put into it every day, how this makes you feel, document any failed attempts along with your emotions, and focus on its successful completion. Once you achieve your goal, document how you feel. Keep journaling for as long as your achievement makes you happy and write down your feelings after the initial reactive feelings fade away.

3 Physics and Human Nature

In the center of this image, is a galaxy that seems to be smiling. Image credit: NASA/ESA

3.1 Laws of Physics Resembling Human Behaviors

Atoms and molecules are ruled by laws of nature. The entire known universe is ruled by laws. What if we study these laws and realize these are also what govern our lives, and even our success and happiness? Human, and several animal societies, are ruled by laws and regulations. What if we are not ruled just by human made-up laws imposed by governments but also by laws of physics? Physics seems to be different from anthropology, biology, psychology, and sociology; however, there are more common characteristics than we can imagine.

There is an abundance of examples of physics laws that can be interpreted in people's everyday lives. No man can live alone, and for this reason societies are created. Similarly, subatomic particles, which are small pieces of matter, cannot live alone, and for this reason quarks form hadrons, the basis of an atom, and atoms make up molecules, and so on. In societies, people have friends and occasionally enemies. They are sometimes attracted to certain people, and they are repelled by others. Some people just prefer to stay neutral toward others. Does this ring a bell? Likewise, particles either attract (when their charges are opposite), or repel (when their charges are the same) other particles. However, there are also neutrons that are neither positively or negatively electrically charged and remain neutral, thus they do not attract or repel other particles.[8] It is all part of the universe!

We all have some common external characteristics, but each one of us is a totally different person. For example, unless there is a physical deformity, we all have two eyes but the look, the shape, the size, and the color differ from person to person. The same applies to every natural element. They all have protons, electrons, and some also have neutrons but essentially, they are totally different regarding their attributes. Even identical twins have personalities that can be entirely different. Just like isotopes. Isotopes are variants of a chemical element, they look alike, they have pretty similar attributes, but their neutrons' number is different. Another common thing between people and physical laws is that there is the ageing of materials phenomenon. Materials, just like people, age. Materials get corroded and oxidized and people get wrinkles.

People perceive their environment with their senses, such as sight, hearing, scent, taste, and touch, or a combination of them, and they move accordingly within their environment. Particles with an electric charge, such as protons and electrons, perceive the electric field where they are situated, and move accordingly in their environment. Neutrons are particles with no electric charge and are like people who have lost one of their senses. Their perception of the environment may be harder, and they have to adapt accordingly.

People need to sleep every night so they can recharge their batteries. Just like people recharging and then being active again, when electrons are charged, they shift from a lower to higher energy level. Similarly to humans though, they "get tired" and their energy level drops.

As Susannah Locke[9] describes, stars maintain their energy with thermonuclear fusion, which is the process that occurs when two atoms combine to make a larger atom, releasing a lot of energy. Fusion happens naturally in stars, when strong pressure and heat fuse hydrogen atoms together, generating helium and energy. When the supply of hydrogen is exhausted, their cores start fusing helium to carbon. We maintain our energy by eating food and drinking water. When we run out of a certain food, we replace it with another.

When a star's core collapses, which happens in less than a second, an explosion called a supernova might occur. The supernova shines brighter than the entire galaxy for a short period of time, usually about three months. This reminds me of crises and scandals on the news. Something collapses, it is all over the news, and people are shocked and in awe, like with the offshore tax haven leak. This news lives in publicity as long as journalists want it to. As soon as journalists find something else to attach to, the news "dies." Scientists recently discovered supernova star iPTF14hls, which erupted continuously for about almost three years while "dying," just like extreme cases of news or scandals that occasionally shock us so much that journalists keep bringing it up again and again.

Let's talk more specifically about some laws and principles.

3.1.1 Principle of Least Action

The principle of least action, also known as the principle of stationary action, states that particles prefer to be in the least possible active situation.

People prefer to do everything with minimum effort. Don't we always try to complete a task as quickly and as easily as possible? When we realize that hard work is required, some people are not that motivated anymore, so we need to push ourselves and stick to our motivations if we want to achieve something.

3.1.2 Theory of Everything

Most physicists hope to discover a single theory that will unify all four fundamental interactions—gravity, strong nuclear force, weak nuclear force, and electromagnetic force—to prove them as various impacts of a single interaction.

More and more people hope to find the perfect mix that makes up happiness. It may be, as previously discussed, a combination of hard work, positive thinking, faith, embracing failure, and appreciating all that is already within our reach. What is your perfect mix?

3.1.3 Newton's Law of Universal Gravitation

Every particle attracts every other particle in the universe with a force that is directly proportional to the product of their masses, and inversely proportional to the square of the distance between their centers of mass. Earth attracts every object, and person, toward its center. Earth is attracted to the Sun. People, respectively, are naturally attracted to light, warmth, and metaphorically speaking, emotional intimacy, happiness, and the truth. The closer the proximity, the better they experience these emotions.

When one gains more mass, it is difficult to remain close to others. Imagine children. As they grow up, they are not in their parents' arms anymore. Equally, when someone grows and works many hours, they don't spend much time with the people close to them. However, when two people have the same big mass, they exert greater force of gravity, and they seem to go hand in hand. Therefore, even though opposites attract, in relationships it seems that people who are like-minded attract to each other and stick together. Accordingly, when the distance between two people increases, the force of gravity decreases. Hence, long-distance friendships and relationships are very hard to work and nurture. Keep this in mind if you are looking for a significant other.

The bigger the mass, the greater the attraction. Think of all the celebrities. They attract their fans, their fans learn as much as possible about the celebrities' lives, and these famous people barely know anything personal from their fans' lives.

Moreover, the closer you are to people, you get to listen to people and learn things. People think differently from each other so you may find new and creative solutions to your problems, or you may learn interesting things and even get interested in new hobbies, studies, jobs, and even professionals and brands, thanks to word-of-mouth.

3.1.4 Newton's Laws of Motion

First law of motion, also known as the principle of inertia, is the resistance of any physical object to any change in its motion. An object either remains at rest or continues to move at a constant velocity, unless a force acts upon it.

We all have habits. Some of them are bad and we may be aware of it. For example, smokers know that smoking is bad for their health, but usually they are not willing to quit unless a great force, such as a grave illness, affects them. I used to be a smoker for about 15 years and I quit smoking when I met my husband who suffered from asthma. Moving in together and me still smoking would probably worsen his asthma, and of course I did not want this for him. It was not that I did not want to quit smoking before I met him. I did, but I never found the right motivation (=the strong force).

The third law of motion is the most famous of all. Every action has an equal and opposite reaction. Whenever something changes, there will always be people who love the change, and people who hate it.

When I was younger, I would change my hair color all the time, from blonde to black, and anything in between. At some point, I even had half blue and half magenta hair. Some people loved it, and some hated it. That is how our world is created. We do not all have the same tastes, therefore we are not programmed to like the same things or people. Similarly when your favorite singer releases a new song, you will love it but there will be many people who will not like it.

3.1.5 Hooke's Law

Hooke's law states that the length that a spring or an object is extended, compressed, or deformed is proportional to the force applied to it.

Respectively, we should not treat everyone the same. We cannot be the same person with friends, family, colleagues, and strangers. That is why we are ready to go to great lengths for the people closer to our heart. Different people have different expectations from us and of course we cannot have the same expectations from everyone. Moreover, there are people who are more elastic, as in flexible, who can accept new concepts more easily than others and keep their minds more open.

Eventually, we are all different from each other, and some people can adapt more or less easily, depending on the timing. For example, someone may be ready to love and be loved while someone else may not. Or someone may be ready to work under pressure while someone else may not under certain circumstances.

3.1.6 Buoyancy

Archimedes' principle of buoyancy states that the upward buoyant force that is exerted on a body immersed in a fluid equals to the weight of the fluid that the body displaces, and pressure increases with depth as a result of the weight of the overlying fluid.

If we press a person or a situation, we change the existing balance and we get a displaced outcome. Think about political tension in a country. When a party pushes for change, the other party reacts equally opposite. In relationships, it is common advice that we should not press someone to do things they do not like, because this may lead the person to leave.

3.1.7 The Law of Refraction

The law of refraction, also known as Snell's law, is the way of predicting how light will bend or refract when it travels from one medium to another. Just like with reflection, refraction involves the angles but unlike reflection, refraction also depends on the media through which the light rays are traveling. Different materials have different refractive indices. Light travels slower through a medium with a high refractive index, and faster through a medium that has a low refractive index.

Equally, everything is perceived differently by different people and we are usually biased in our understanding of others because we judge them with what is on our minds. That is why we need to be good listeners and make sure we understand what others say. Moreover, we need to understand that ideas are not adopted at the same time by everyone. Some people want and need more time before they make a decision and a choice.

3.1.8 Chaos Theory

Chaos theory states that certain systems that are very sensitive can be affected by a very small change and, in turn, behave completely differently. Chaos theory entails the butterfly effect. A butterfly may flap its wings in Chicago and a hurricane is caused in Paris after a few weeks. Small changes may have a big impact and this is why the weather forecast lasts only for a few days. Even if the best computer could measure the weather, a small change, like a butterfly flapping its wings, could create wind and change the weather.

Just like chaos theory, a small step at a time can start an immense transformation. When we set goals, we need to take one step at a time and focus, because a small action can change our entire lives. Do not forget that just like the chaos theory is of time-dependent nature, our efforts generate results over time.

3.1.9 Theory of General Relativity

General relativity is Einstein's theory connecting space and time, and it is based on the principle of equivalence. An example is that two people, one in an elevator on Earth and the other in an elevator in outer space accelerating at a certain speed (9.8 m/s^2), will each observe the same behavior of an object they drop from their hand. The object will accelerate to the floor at the same speed (9.8 m/s^2) in both cases, making it impossible for either person to distinguish whether or not they are at rest in a gravitational field or accelerating. This is a matter of perspective. A third objective party can distinguish the difference between these two people but these two people are unable to understand what is going on.

I like to call this "subjective presbyopia." One can see and realize someone else's problems, mistakes, motivations, among other things, while they usually cannot realize their own problems, mistakes, and motivations. For example, you may have met a couple that you have observed, and it is clear to you that these people should break up for a number of reasons, but they deny to admit the problem and end up breaking up years later.

3.1.10 Absolute Zero Temperature

Absolute zero is the temperature at which particles are at their lowest energy levels. Absolute zero in Kelvin degrees equals to –273.15 degrees Celsius and –459.67 degrees Fahrenheit. Some people think that particles lose all energy and stop moving at absolute zero but this is incorrect. Matter is just sitting at its quantum mechanical ground state, which is the point of lowest internal energy.

When people suffer from depression, a mental breakdown, or a burnout, it may seem that they have no energy, but the truth is that they are at their lowest energy point, and they need to rest, relax, and take care of themselves so they can recover and recharge their batteries.

3.1.11 Entropy

Entropy measures the amount of energy unavailable to do any work and, in thermodynamics, it characterizes the unavailability of a system to convert thermal energy into mechanical and, therefore, kinetic energy.

We all need to have energy in order to do any work. The lower our level of energy, the less things we can do. Sometimes, when we are physically, mentally, or emotionally exhausted, even simple tasks seem impossible to be conducted. Since food gives us energy, I would guess this is why comfort food gives us energy to do simple tasks when we feel down.

3.1.12 Conservation of Energy

Conservation of energy means that energy is neither created or destroyed, but it is converted from one form into another. Even though energy is not infinite, its manifestations are.

When we are physically and mentally healthy, we have an amount of energy that we choose how to channel. We can work, play, volunteer, do chores and housework, or a bunch of other things. As we discussed in the first chapter, we all have needs that change depending on what we have already done and achieved and it is our choice how we prioritize them.

3.1.13 Mach's Principle

If you stand in a room with your arms free at your sides, and you start spinning, your arms will be pulled away from your body. This is happening because of conservation of energy, and motion is subjective, and it is only meaningful when it is measured against a point of reference.

We need to set personal goals and see how we have proceeded against these goals and not against someone else with similar or identical goals. If for example one wants to lose 10lb and sets this as a goal with a friend who wants to lose the same amount of weight, we should never compare against each other's weekly results. One may need ten weeks in order to lose 10lb while another may need five weeks. The point is that we stick to our goal, we work hard, and observe our own progression instead of comparing our progress to someone else's progress.

3.2 Determinism and Free Will

Determinism suggests that certain physics laws always apply, and a specific cause will always lead to a specific outcome. This is also known as cause-and-effect. However, there are laws that are probabilistic, which means the outcome depends on the odds according to the cause.

Determinism is different from fatalism. Fatalism suggests that at least some events are destined to occur no matter what we do, but not because of laws of nature, but because of the will of the gods, or some teleological aspect of the universe.

However, quantum physics, also known as quantum mechanics, is known for its indeterminacy. Quantum means "how much" in Latin, and describes a specific amount of energy while mechanics is the branch of physics dealing with motion. Quantum mechanics is about probabilities in a period of time and not about deterministic outcomes.

Many philosophers and physicists have been wondering whether there is free will. Do we live a deterministic or indeterministic life?

Carlo Rovelli, a physics professor at Aix-Marseille University, suggests that "if human freedom to choose was reducible to quantum indeterminism, then we should conclude that human choices are strictly regulated by the chance. Which is the opposite of the idea of freedom of choice." He goes on and says that we need to accept a definition for free will and he gives the following example: "I can decide whether to declare or not some revenues to the IRS. This is a free choice. What does this mean? First it means that I am not forced to make a choice by external constraints. For example, there is no law that states that I get the money only after I have declared it. If so I would have no choice. Secondly, there is no IRS inspector watching me, in which case I would not have choice either. I am free to choose to be honest or dishonest."[10]

Every day, we assess the advantages and disadvantages of both simple and complicated situations, and we make decisions based on both external factors that are out of our control and internal factors that are based on our moral code.

According to Rovelli, human behavior is determined by something like a biological software, and our brain is a machine that works in a probabilistic manner based on statistical elements. My take on this is that this software can be reprogrammed and altered using the right tools and techniques.

Twin siblings may experience the same external factors and internal states, such as education, upbringing, and emotions, but they may behave differently. Our brains have millions of synapses, passing signals, and we have not yet figured out how everything in our brain works. The evolution of the universe is determined but we still do not know how and why we think.

However, the fact that the journey of every individual cannot be determined does not mean that their path does not exist as a probability.

3.3 Conclusion

Neuroscience of free will studies topics related to free will using neuroscience. In 2008, an experiment was conducted by scientists using brain scanning technology. It was found that a person's brain seems to commit to certain decisions before the person becomes aware of having made them.[11] However, this only predicted actions with 60% accuracy, therefore it is not conclusive but it seems like there is free will and we have the ability to shape our future. Otherwise the percentage of the accurate predicted actions would have been near to 100%, and we could probably conclude that life is deterministic. However, it appears that life is not deterministic, there is free will, and everyone is responsible for reaching their goals, and thus achieving success and happiness.

All of the aforementioned physics laws are of deterministic nature so I believe that it is extremely important to start paying attention to situations and circumstances with these laws in mind. When we recall all this knowledge, we can judge both people and situations better and make more educated decisions since we get a lot more insights and information when we observe patterns and behaviors.

Good decisions are the basis of success and provide solutions that are logical. A good decision maker should be realistic, flexible, and open-minded, and should not be afraid of trying new things. So try physics and move forward. Think positive, with no stress or worries!

The more physicists discover, the more complicated universe seems to be, and the more difficult for people to understand how it works. Reality is often not what we perceive. We thought there were three dimensions but quantum physicists now talk about 10, 11, or even 26 dimensions and talk about probabilities instead of determinism.[12] Scientists keep measuring and testing, and that is what we should do too.

The law of attraction should be tested and measured by each one of us to see whether it works or not. If we indeed attract what we want, we just need to measure the results, even if we are not fully able to understand how it works. Remember what Albert Einstein said "Imagination is more important than knowledge. For knowledge is limited, whereas imagination embraces the entire world, stimulating progress, giving birth to evolution."

So, to sum up, remember that according to this interpretation of the laws of physics, we need to:

1. Push ourselves and stick to our motivations if we want to achieve something.
2. Identify our personal happiness mix.
3. Long-distance relationships and friendships need very hard work.
4. When something changes, there will be people loving and people hating the change. We do not all like the same things or people.
5. We are ready to go to great lengths for the people closer to our heart.
6. There are people who can accept new concepts more easily than others.
7. We need to be good listeners and make sure we understand what others communicate.

8. When we set goals, we need to take one step at a time, because a small action can change our lives.
9. Most of us suffer from "subjective presbyopia" and have a hard time recognizing our problems compared to other people's problems.
10. When people suffer from depression, a mental breakdown, or a burnout, they need to rest and take care of themselves so they can recharge their batteries.
11. We need to set personal goals and see how we have proceeded against these goals instead of comparing ourselves to someone else's progress.

3.4 Assignment for Reflection

Write at least two examples of physics laws applying to your life at the moment, and think of what should be done or how these situations should be dealt with in order to get the desired outcome.

4 Achieving Success

Learning about the laws of physics helps us in making more educated choices. We see how our known world operates and we operate accordingly so that we decrease the chances of failure. However, our life is a resultant force obtained by a combination of forces, so our happiness and success depend on physics and psychology, among other factors.

The biologist Dr. Bruce Lipton said that our fate depends on the pictures we set our mind to. He claims that the pictures we hold in our mind are translated by our brain into chemistry that complements these pictures. This chemistry is then put in our blood and our body responds to these pictures in our mind accordingly.[13]

Cells can be in either a growth mode or in a protection mode. They cannot be in both modes at the same time. For example, when we have a picture of fear in our mind, our brain releases cortisol, our stress hormone, because our body is in protection mode. When we want to achieve success, we need to be in growth mode, and we need to know who we are and what success is for us.

4.1 Your Values and Motivations

Values are principles that we consider important in life. They are these little voices in our head saying "that's right" or "absolutely not" when we do or think about various things. Fortunately, or unfortunately, each one of us has developed our own ethical code consisting of our values. Identifying your personal values will help you tremendously in understanding your behavior and motivations, and it will ultimately lead you to a more fulfilling life. To identify your values, ask yourself the following questions:

1. What type of person do you want to be?

As a romantic partner, as a child, as a parent, as a relative, as a professional, as a friend, as a sibling, as part of a community. Keep in mind that you may not be the same person in every role, and this is absolutely fine. You can be a very serious professional in a work environment and a child at heart playing games and laughing all the time at home. Or you can be a loyal friend but not a loyal employee because your boss is terrible or your job is not fulfilling or your salary is not decent, and so on. It is time to decide who you want to be in every role. Nobody will judge you for your choices so you have to be honest with yourself. Remember that as you grow older, or as the more you develop yourself, you can adopt different values and change your behaviors in every role.

2. What is the most important thing to stand for?

Is it family? Is it money? Maybe friendship, a favorite team, or religion? Or a million other things. Find below some of the most common values that people share. This list is not exhaustive so you may have more important things to stand for that are not mentioned.

Acceptance: Recognition of your value, being respected for who you are.

Achievement: Goals accomplishment, personal development.

Adrenaline rush: Experiencing new opportunities, meeting new people.

Change: Lack of routine, element of surprise.

Family: Spending time with your partner, children, parents, extended family.

Financial success: Earning a high income, accumulating wealth.

Friendship: Having good friends who stand by you and you stand by them.

Happiness: Appreciating what is there, satisfaction, contentment.

Health: Maintaining physical and mental health.

Helping others: Offering help to friends, family, and the community, collaboration.

Honesty: Respect for both written and unwritten rules, sincerity, reliability.

Independence: Freedom of speech and choices, autonomy to self-serve.

Influence: Having an impact on others, being famous.

Inner peace: Feeling tranquility, self-respect.

Justice: Being fair, battling for equality.

Love: Being loved and loving deeply and purely.

Loyalty: Being faithful and dedicated to people and/or any cause you serve.

Physical activity: Staying in good shape no matter your age.

Retribution: Retaliation for something someone has done to you or a loved one.

Safety: Feeling safe and ensuring your loved ones' safety.

Spirituality: Following spiritual or religious beliefs.

Which of the abovementioned values are part of your everyday life and resonate with you? You have now identified your values so you can now focus on the things you can do to improve your life.

Keep in mind that you may need to adopt appropriate behaviors that fit your personality traits. If you want to battle for equality, for example, but you are introvert or shy or have social phobia, going to a pride parade may not be the right route for you. However, you can start a blog and write about LGBTQ people's rights and increase awareness by sharing your knowledge online.

Accordingly, if you want to prioritize physical activity but you hate going to the gym, you can try something alternative. I started working out with aerial acrobatics when I was 32, and a classmate of mine was 53 years old, so you are never too old to start something new that will make you feel better.

Once you know what you want from your life and who you want to be, you will cease being confused and you will start planning your steps, thus pursuing your goals will be easier than ever.

4.2 Mindset and Attitude

As previously said, "What you think is what you become" and the difference between who you are and who you want to be is driven by your mindset.

Our upbringing, our environment, our education, our religion, and our experiences form our beliefs, thoughts, and opinions. In other words, we set our mind to these beliefs. Our mindset then shapes our actions and reactions. It is sort of like a habit that we are "addicted" to. On the other hand, an attitude is our behavior that is driven by our mindset. In other words, it is our reaction and response to various events.

Developing the right mindset is essential in order to succeed. While we can change both our attitude and mindset, it is easier to change our attitude first. Although it may sound easy to you to change your attitude or mindset, there are many people who think it is impossible. For example, there are people who claim that it is too late to go back to school or change career paths. Truth is that it is never too late for most things. If you believe you can do it, you can do it, but if you believe you cannot do it because you are old, because you have other priorities, or because of a bunch of other reasons, you will never do it. The truth is as simple as that.

My neighbor, Melina, is a 60-year-old lady. When she was young, she wanted to become a veterinarian but she did not become one. She always loved animals and she has always had a lot of happy cats and dogs at home. Melina did not work. She became a stay-at-home mom to raise her three kids. Her kids grew up and left home to study. Two years ago, Melina went back to school, she studied, and she became a veterinary assistant. She now works at a vet clinic.

My mother started working when I was one year old. She was a court official but she did not like her job as she found it boring and she wanted something to excite her. When she was 40, with two small children, she went back to school and, a year later, she became a middle school teacher. When she was 68, and already retired, she attended a course about fixing computer motherboards.

That's right, you are never too old to do changes that will bring you happiness.

4.2.1 Positive Attitude

Positive thinking is an attitude. Specifically, it is the attitude that increases success. We usually think first and act later. So, start thinking who you want to be and become this person. When you are not productive, focus on your skills and abilities. Focus on your goal. Stop thinking about your fears and worries. Stop thinking about dystopian future cases that may never happen, and instead focus on your success.

Recall your values and think of what inspired you to pursue your goal. You need to have your motivation clear in your mind, so you can take courage and energy every time you draw back to your old self. Once you become self-conscious of the fact that you are the master of your feelings and your thoughts, you will be able to start thinking positively.

When we talk about our goals and dreams, and make plans about how we will achieve them, we feel happy. When we feel happy, our brain releases the four main feel-good hormones—endorphins, oxytocin, serotonin, and dopamine—that often act as pain relievers and happiness boosters. According to many medical doctors, positive thinking reduces depression and stress levels.

Remember that optimism is what distinguishes happy from unhappy people. Optimists go after what they want and they embrace failure. Every cloud has a silver lining so even when things do not go as planned or as well as expected, look for the silver lining. Our brain can concentrate on one thing at a time. So every time you think of something negative, or you are anxious, or nervous, just concentrate on a happy thought and you will see a major difference.

Nobody has ever claimed that positive thinking opens all doors immediately. That would be a lie. You may adopt positive thinking and still find obstacles, and still fail at times. But this time, you will learn from your mistakes and you will see clearly which areas you need to improve. You will gain control and will feel empowered so you succeed next time. Change your attitude and then change your mindset.

If you are wondering what positive attitudes are, there are many. A positive attitude is when you try to make the people around you happy with a compliment. It is when you are kind to people you do not know. Other examples of positive attitudes include, among others, appreciating all you have and being happy with it, being happy with someone else's victories, cheering people up when they are feeling down, embracing failure and learning from it, and never giving up on fighting for your values.

Keep in mind that you may feel sad and hurt at times, even if you have adopted positive thinking. You do not need to hide and suppress these negative emotions. They are absolutely normal. You may cry or release them in any other healthy way. This is fine and nobody will judge you. The most important factor in positive thinking is for it to be real. Do not pretend that you are completely happy if something tragic has happened. Let it out. Only then will you be able to go back to concentrating on the silver lining.

4.2.2 Success Mindset

The success mindset will give you the flexibility to pinpoint your options and the plans you need to make in order to move forward to your goal. What does it mean to have a success mindset? It means that you have a growth mindset. It means that you believe you can become the best version of yourself and achieve your goals with hard work. It also means that you develop or improve certain traits, like those listed below.

Ambition: Have ambitions. Make dreams even if they sound unrealistic. These are your motivational force. Pursue them. The more challenging they are, the harder you will work for them. Keep the focus and remain disciplined.

Patience: Be patient. Successful people work hard to move ahead, but they are patient and can wait until they reach their goals. It is not procrastination. It is that they do not give up.

Positivity: Be positive, brave, and active. Be a realistic optimist, face your fears, and find the motivation to make the changes you want. Embrace change and flexibility. Remember to laugh and play! Laughter and playing keeps the small child we have inside alive, and this makes us feel and look younger!

Problem-solving: There are two kinds of people. Problem bringers and problem solvers. Problem bringers usually cause trouble or just talk too much and do nothing. Successful people are problem solvers and get a lot of things done. They try ideas and they offer up solutions.

Self-awareness: Know yourself. Identify your strengths and your weak spots and work on both. Respect yourself and your values, rely on yourself, and understand that we all make mistakes. Failure is not the end. Get advantage of your mistakes and learn from failure so that you become better.

Self-leadership: Gain control of your thoughts and feelings. Do not panic and do not snap inappropriately. Remember that we rarely think the same way with other people. Listen to others, and show compassion even if you do not agree with them. We all want to be heard, so become a good listener.

4.3 How Can You Change?

Our mindset can hinder us or help us achieve our potential. This is why we need to be aware of our mindset and switch to a growth mindset if we have not already done so. Become self-aware of your emotional state and understand why you do what you do, and why you feel the way you feel about everything. Identify the reasons and reasoning behind your behavior and responses, and accept that your mindset may need adjustments. Remember that it is fine to adjust your mindset so that it starts serving you in order to reach happiness and success.

Many people are stuck in the past and cannot change their mindset. It is time to face the present and open up for the future. We may not be responsible for tragic events that have taken place in the world or in our own life, and that have affected us, but we are 100% responsible for how we will deal with them and for any traumas that will stick with us for the rest of our life. When we stick to the past, we victimize ourselves, and lose control of our life. However, we should always keep in mind that we are responsible for our actions toward success and happiness. You need to make sure that you do not turn into a monster, snapping out to innocent people, and please do not let your traumatic past define you.

Many people may not be stuck in the past, but they keep comparing themselves to others. What is great for me may be bad for someone else. Let us think of celebrities for a moment. Many people wish they could date a famous singer, for example. Said singer may have a hidden addiction, like alcoholism, and therefore is a bad dating choice for someone wishing to date them but wants, at the same time, to lead a healthy lifestyle. Or this singer may love playing video games instead of going to clubs. Is it still the perfect match for someone who wants to dance all Saturday night?

When we are not involved in a situation and only know bits and pieces of the truth, we make assumptions and tend to be jealous or even envious of things that would never really make us happy. We may think that our acquaintance is in a perfect romantic relationship but when this person is behind closed doors, they may be completely disrespected or neglected by their partner. So we should never compare ourselves to others because they only let us know the bits that they want us to know about their personal lives.

You may see someone and think they are rich because they drive an expensive car or live in a big house. How would you feel if you found out that this person lives in a cold house because they do not want to spend money on gas to heat their house? How would you feel if you discovered that someone who had purchased the latest smartphone model actually couldn't afford to pay their own bills for the next three months and lives off their parents' income? These are two very real examples I have witnessed. Never assume that the part of the truth that you do not know is what you imagine. So what do you need to do in order change?

1.   Identify your strengths and weaknesses

a. Identify your strengths. List your strengths at work, in relationships, hobbies, and anything else you may think of, such as housework, and write an example where you last used your strengths successfully. Now write what you can do so that you can improve these strengths even more.

b. Now identify your weaknesses. List your weaknesses at work, in relationships, hobbies, and anything else you can think of, and write an example where you did not manage to do something successfully. Remember that nobody has to read your list so you can be completely honest with yourself. Now write what you can do so you can improve these weaknesses.

2.   Adopt new habits!

a. Start a gratitude journal. Keep a note at the end of every day about something that happened, or someone you talked to and made you feel gratitude. It may be that you saw a butterfly in the park, or someone you called, or something you did, and so on. You can also start a mental journal. Instead of writing, just lie in bed and think of at least a positive thing that happened to you, before you fall asleep.

b. Stop looking at the world in black and white. Check the gray color. Listen to others, and understand their ideas and points, even if you do not agree. You may realize there are things you did not know or never thought about. Listening to other people's perspectives does not harm us. On the contrary, it can help us a lot.

c. Think outside the box and feed your inner child. A few years ago, on Spanish TV, they asked a few adults what they would like to physically change, if they could change absolutely anything. Answers were along the lines "I wish I could be taller" or "I wish I could be blonde" and so on. Then they asked kids the same question and answers were tremendously different. Kids would say "I wish I could fly" or "I wish I could be invisible." Look around you. People who remain children at heart always look younger.

d. Focus on what you already have right now. Do you have a place to call home, even if someone is currently hosting you? Do you have food? Do you have someone to talk to? If you have at least one of these, then you have a lot more than many people out there. Celebrate!

e. Decide to be happy. Start looking at the glass as half full instead of half empty. Look on the bright side and always look for the silver lining. Yes, it is a choice you can make, and you can make it right now.

f. Embrace failure. We all make mistakes and we all fail at times. The point is that we learn from our mistakes and we never repeat them. Find solutions that will work.

g. Start your day with positive affirmations. When you repeat something, you end up believing it so keep telling yourself a couple of mantras like "I am a warrior and I always rise" or "I decide to be happy." Stop using negative phrases like "I'm useless."

h. Convert negative thoughts to positive thoughts. Stop being cruel to yourself. Be kind to yourself, appreciate your efforts, stop minimizing your success, focus on how you will overcome obstacles, and develop yourself further. If you start paying attention to the positives, your brain will learn and it will start doing this automatically.

i. Relax. Breathe to relax. Watch something funny, listen to your favorite music, dance, read, exercise, go hiking, travel, meet people you like, do something that you love, and have fun.

j. Restore your faith in humanity. Observe the goodness in people. One morning, I was walking my dog and I saw from far away an old man falling down on the street. By the time I'd reached the elderly man, there were people surrounding him, someone sat by his side and held him, because he was dizzy, and another brought him a bottle of water. Be like this. Help people with no expectations. If you have time, volunteer for a cause you believe in.

4.4 How Your Environment Helps or Obstructs You

Assess the people around you. Are they positive or negative? How do you feel every time you meet them? You may realize there is one pattern when you meet positive people and another, completely different pattern, when you meet negative people.

When we surround ourselves with negative people, we tend to focus on negativity subconsciously. You do not want to focus on negativity, do you? You want to talk to people who, just like you, focus on nice things and share happy stories. You want to convert negative thoughts into positive ones so you need to stop spending time with negative people. By spending less time with negative people, you grow a more positive outlook on life.

Remember that you do not have to deal with negative people around you. You are not obliged to do so. It may be an old friend who became grumpy, a mean colleague, or even a family member and it can be hard to deal with at times, but you really need to get rid of the negativity in your life. Once you realize someone is negative, you need to accept that it is fine to say goodbye. Always make sure you protect yourself.

Negative people share some common traits so it is easy to recognize them. Remember that a negative person is always like this. It is not a phase. It is normal that we sometimes feel up and down, feel pessimism even, but negative people never have ups.

1. They are pessimists. They cannot see the good around them, and they always think of the worst possible scenario or outcome.
2. They are the victim. They love complaining, they never assume responsibility, they and never work on solutions. It is always other people's fault or their bad luck.
3. They are jealous of other people's achievements. They will never be happy for you and will never be able to celebrate your success.
4. They suck your energy. Every time you meet them, you feel emotionally drained and physically exhausted.

Negative people stall our development because they affect our way of thinking. They exhaust us, and when we are tired it is easier to start focusing on bad things. Life is too short to spend it on people who do not make you happy. Negative people always focus on the bad things and will discourage you because they do not know how to support others. Every time you tell them something new and exciting, they will diminish it and make you feel bad. For example, you may tell them you lost 10lbs, and they will tell you something along the lines of "the first 10lbs are the easy ones, you have to try now" because they want to diminish your effort.

On the other hand, surrounding yourself with positive people will lead you to a whole new level. Positive people are kind with you, compliment you, encourage you and, most of all, they believe in you. They support you when you need help, they make you laugh, and they become a source of inspiration and motivation for those who try to adopt a positive mindset. They will be happy for you and celebrate your success no matter its size.

If you are looking for positive people to mingle with, just be open and show your new positive version. We meet people all the time so start building relationships. Go out there and smile! Listen to people, respect them, be kind, do not judge them, make them smile, and help them if they need your help and you will see that all of a sudden, you are surrounded by positive people!

Always keep in mind what Plato said about friendship: "People are like dirt. They can either nourish you and help you grow as a person, or they can stunt your growth and make you wilt and die."

4.5 Succeed in Work

My significant experience in Human Resource Management and Talent Management helped me understand how can once succeed in work. First impressions do matter so always be on time, appropriately dressed, and make sure you never miss deadlines.

I have met a few terrible bosses who treat their subordinates poorly and even bully them, but this is not the optimal way to get things done so the following is a compiled list of what you should be doing in order to climb the ladder in a company, if this is what you are after.

1. Build relationships. Be friendly with your colleagues and your boss and show genuine interest. Bond with your team and make sure you always have each other's back. Have your lunch break with them, go for a drink after work, play games and sports with them, and ultimately build trust without gossiping or judging anyone. Remember that your sense of humor is great ammunition, because everyone wants to laugh and release tension. Of course, good manners also help so "please" and "thank you" are more than welcome. If your colleagues trust you, they will ask for your help and they will appreciate you even more. If your boss trusts you, they will assign you more worthwhile tasks and they will keep an eye on you for future succession.

2. Be a great two-way communicator. Always communicate openly and make sure everyone understands what you want to convey. Also make sure you are a good listener. Albert Mehrabian, Professor of Psychology at the University of California, studied nonverbal messages and he found that only 7% of our communication is verbal, 55% of our communication is body language, and 38% consists of the tone of voice.[14] This is why you need to pay attention to the person talking to you without checking your phone and you should always maintain eye contact. In the end, recap and make sure you understood exactly what they meant. Keep in mind that you need to show self-control and emotional intelligence no matter how extreme your speaker's views are. Even if you completely disagree with your speaker, compassion and understanding are great qualities to cultivate and show, especially for a future leader, so offer support.

3. Add value. Take initiatives and speak up in meetings. If you are shy or introverted, work on these traits so that you find the courage to start talking more. Stop stressing if you are in a room with higher management. They all want the same thing—to increase productivity and sales. Show everyone that you have innovative ideas and you can add value to the company.

4. Keep learning. You may have excellent credentials in your field but things change and advance all the time. Learn about the industry and the world, attend workshops, courses, and conferences and do not be afraid of learning new skills. Always welcome feedback without taking it personally, and use it as an opportunity to improve.

5. Solve problems. Many employees talk to their boss about their work problems. Focus on bringing solutions instead of problems. If you have a problem and want to talk about it, always proactively think of at least one solution to suggest. If you do not have a problem, but see an issue, bring it up along with possible solutions.

6. Ask. If you need help, ask for it. If you do not know how you are supposed to do something, ask for guidance. Ask questions. It is always preferred to ask for help and make sure you complete something successfully. If you want to make a change, talk about it. If you want a promotion, work hard and ask for it. If you get the promotion, celebrate and work even harder to rise even higher, if this is what you truly want.

7. Motivate others. Support the people around you, encourage them, and if they ask, give them your honest and kind feedback. Ask them if you can help them somehow and do not be afraid of helping them succeed.

Your boss will notice that you have leadership skills and the people around you will be willing to go the extra mile when you become their boss.

8. Record your success and show off. You have worked hard and have achieved success. Do not hesitate to bring it up if your boss does not do so. Talk about the challenges you faced and the additional effort you had to put it and make sure everyone surrounding you has heard about your success, including higher management who need to know who you are and what you have achieved if you want to climb the ladder.

9. Be a good negotiator. Learn how to negotiate both internally for your sake and externally with vendors and customers. You want your customers happy, your company happy, but most of all yourself with a decent salary and a decent work-life balance. Negotiation is related to the ability of persuasion. You need to have great and rational arguments in order to persuade those around you.

10. Be positive. It may be a hard day at work, a deadline may be close, you may work overtime, but you should keep your positive attitude so you can perform under pressure and show that you can handle stress and keep your cool.

Some of the aforementioned tips also work for self-employed people. Build relationships, be a great communicator, add value to your customers, keep learning, and be positive. On top of these, remember to look for new customers on a regular basis. Build your portfolio and go out there. Stop only when people learn your name and what you do, if you want to grow your business.

Are you a freelancer? Create profiles on every freelance website, approach companies, build your website, and invest in free advertising, such as quality content on your website, if you do not have the required budget for paid advertising. Do not give up and you will eventually increase your clientele.

4.6 Succeed in Relationships

Relationships are the way people are connected. They can be romantic relationships with a partner or a spouse, friendships, or relationships with family members. There are also social interactions with acquaintances and colleagues, but in this section, we focus on close relationships. Close relationships have many common characteristics and they require patience. Read below what you need to do in order to create successful bonds.

1. Build trust. Be open and talk about your likes and dislikes, your worries and accomplishments, as well as your views on a variety of topics. Be patient and the other person will eventually open up as well, if you are honest. Remember to be a good listener and give your undivided attention in order to understand what you hear. Most of all, never gossip about them, be sincere, and keep your word if you make promises.

2. Be there for this person. Be available and make room not only when you want to talk and share something but also when the other person needs you. Always support and encourage them, show compassion and kindness, and respect them and their opinions. Never hurt them intentionally, and never do what you do not want people to do to you.

3. Accept them. Understand that the other person will probably not change, at least radically, so accept them and appreciate them for who they are and let them be whoever they want to be. Preferences may change but the core of a person will probably remain the same. Show gratitude for having them in your life and focus on their positive qualities. You can show your appreciation with kind words, offering help with a chore, and even a well-thought gift. Remember that a gift does not need to be expensive. It may be a handmade birthday cake or a photo collage, or anything else that you put effort into.

4. Have a positive attitude. Lift people up, laugh at their jokes, respect them, and do not judge or attack them. Do not take this person and their actions for granted if you want to build a strong bond. If you are wrong, apologize and show you mean it. We all make mistakes, it is not necessarily a big deal, but you need to learn from your mistakes. Remember to have fun and celebrate each other's victories!

5. Be a team. Do not compete. Work together instead and motivate each other on a common purpose. Help each other so you both succeed. Stand together against challenges and mean people, and have each other's back.

In romantic relationships, we usually invest more time and effort, since we tend to spend more time with our partner, especially if we live together. However before investing more time, pay attention to the way you feel when you are not with your significant other, once your honeymoon period is over, usually after a few months. If you feel strong, optimistic, and full of energy, it seems like it is really a relationship you should invest in. If you do not miss your partner at all, if you feel down for prolonged periods of time, or if you feel negative emotions, especially caused by your relationship, assess the situation objectively, perhaps with someone else's help, whether it is someone you trust or a professional coach.

All of the aforementioned tips are to be followed in romantic relationships as well, but we need to follow a few more so that we can lay the foundation for a great romantic relationship.

1. Prioritize your long-term partner. Express your needs and desires clearly and not with cues. Spend time together and always be available if your partner needs you. Set long-term goals and use "we" so that your partner understands you are committed and you see a future with them, provided that this is what you want. Always make sure that you share more with your partner than anyone else and make them your best friend.

2. Express your love. Tell your partner you love them and do things for them. Make breakfast or put a little love note in the pocket of their coat so they can find it later. Be affectionate, hold them, kiss them, and hug them. Compliment them and tell them how beautiful you find them.

3. Remain calm. When you argue or disagree with your partner, remain calm. Do not shout or fight. If you need some time, go for a walk and come back later so you can solve the problem in a peaceful manner. Respect your partner and make sure you both learn from your arguments and you both assume responsibility.

4. Start something together. Hit the gym, play games, watch a TV series, or anything else that you both enjoy doing. At the same time, accept that both you and your partner may need some alone time. If you feel insecure

about it, talk to your partner so they can reassure you that it is just a need and nothing you should worry about.

5. Accept that great relationships need work and there will be problems that you will need to solve. Nobody is perfect and your relationship will probably not look like a romantic comedy. Work on yourself so that you feel good and this, in turn, will make you feel good about the relationship as well.

Finally remember that you will not find your soulmate easily, but once you do, you will know. It does not matter if you have had bad experiences. You can still work on a good relationship. Just remember to learn from your past mistakes and also from other people's mistakes. You do not need to do what your parents or siblings do or did.

4.7 Conclusion

Remember that success is the accomplishment of a goal or a purpose. We frequently set goals and reach them. This does not necessarily mean we will feel fulfilled or happy because we are successful. We may be happy for a while, but then we may realize that our goal was not what we truly wanted. After all, we are all so different from each other and we are not all made to do and feel the same things. I may love playing with my 90lb dog, but my friend, Lina, is afraid of dogs and this would never make her happy, even if she managed to toss him the ball and play with him. She would be successful in playing and even conquering her fear for a moment but she would not be happy.

Stop wasting your valuable time pursuing things or relationships with people who give you nothing but negative emotions or emptiness. Keep in mind that you are the only one responsible for your choices and responses to everything, so only you hold the steering wheel. Drive toward success.

4.8 Assignment for Reflection

The following exercise helps you realize what motivates you. Write down a goal you wish to achieve. Think and find the reason why you want to achieve the specific goal. If, for example, you want to lose weight, is it because you want to feel inner peace? Is it for health reasons or to feel more attractive? This is the value motivating you.

Once you have answered the questions above, brainstorm, and start breaking your goal down into (a) must have, (b) nice to have, and (c) not important. If you want to lose weight, you can write something like the following:

Must have	Nice to have	Not important
Hire a dietitian	Hire a personal trainer	Hire a cook
Running shoes	Yoga mattress	Calorie-counting app

There may be anything in these lists and they can be as long as you want. You may even want to expand and write that you must have a specific brand of running shoes, and so on. Once you are done with this list, you need to prioritize your must-haves and create a top three. For example, these are the things to consider when you decide to start losing weight.

Keep in mind that you need to take under consideration your motivation, your environment, and your personality traits that may help or hinder your efforts. For example:

Motivation: What will make you want to lose weight and stick to your plan? Do you want to be healthy? Do you want to find yourself attractive? Do you want to seduce someone?

Environment: Do people close to you eat unhealthy foods and is there a chance that they will tempt you? Can you stop going out for dinner and drinks for as long as it is required? Maybe you can just go out once a week instead of thrice?

Personality traits: What are your relevant traits? Are you patient? Are you disciplined? If not, how will you improve these traits?

5 Achieving Happiness

5.1 Knowing Yourself

So far, we have talked about physics and psychology regarding achieving success. How about achieving happiness? What is happiness? Happiness is a mental state experiencing positive emotions such as satisfaction and contentment. Remember that what makes someone else happy can be entirely different from what makes YOU happy.

Oftentimes, we prioritize other people's needs over our own. We even change some things so the people around us like us more (or so we think) and we may end up losing our true identity. As Aristotle said, "Knowing yourself is the beginning of all wisdom." Be honest to yourself about who you are and do not forget who you want to be. Only once you have learnt who you are, you can move forward and reach happiness.

Knowing yourself is not just about your favorite food or music. It is about understanding your deeper self. It is about bringing to surface your insecurities, your strengths, your weaknesses, your beliefs, your values, your priorities, and ultimately your purpose in life.

Know who you are, what you like and dislike, and why you do the things you do. Reflect on past decisions that significantly affected your life, and understand why you took them at the time. Recall your childhood because a big part of our behavior depends on our childhood and see how it has impacted your decisions and relationships. As discussed in the previous chapter, spend time to understand your core values, especially those driving your motivations and dedicate time in identifying your strengths and weaknesses.

Define who and what matters to you, and what your dreams and aspirations are. Dreams are important because they act as a motivation, so work hard to make them come true. Find your life mission. Do you want people to remember you in the future? If yes, for what? How do you imagine your future? How do you want to treat those around you? How do you want others to treat you?

Answer the following questions to learn more about yourself. Make sure you are open and always true to yourself. Only if you find where you stand, and have faith in yourself, will you be able to excel and achieve happiness.

1. What are ten (either positive or negative) traits that define you?
2. What is your highest value that you would never negotiate over?
3. What are your self-limiting beliefs?
4. How do you feel about your parents?
5. Do you believe in fate?
6. What are your strengths and weaknesses?
7. What are your goals?
8. What motivates you?
9. What are you grateful for?
10. What do you admire in others?
11. What are the things you feel insecure about?
12. What do you worry about?
13. What are your beliefs in religion and politics?
14. If a relationship or job makes you unhappy, do you stay or leave and why?
15. If you could have a wish granted, what would it be and why?
16. What is the thing that makes you the proudest?
17. When was one time you failed but learnt from it?

18. Do you need someone else to make you happy?
19. Do you care what others think?
20. How do you see yourself in 20 years?

As one of my favorite quotes from a TV series goes, "If you're gonna look at yourself, really look in the mirror, you gotta admit who you are. But not just to yourself, you gotta admit it to everybody else."[15] This is the manifestation of self-awareness and the path to self-actualization—which is happiness.

5.2 Knowing Others

Laozi said "Knowing others is wisdom, knowing yourself is enlightenment." We just talked about knowing ourselves. How about knowing others? Knowing others can be a lot easier if we build trust so that others can be honest with us. As we mentioned in the third chapter, "subjective presbyopia" helps us see more clearly and easily why others do the things they do and how they feel. It is usually a lot more difficult to recognize why we do the things we do and how we sincerely feel. For example, we may look at somebody and realize what they have, what they have achieved, and what they should be grateful for, or what they should change, while at the same time, it may be hard, or even impossible, to do the same for us.

However, keep in mind that there are times that we cannot be objective and truly know someone. When we fall in love, or when we identify parts of ourselves with someone, we tend to think that this specific person is perfect and would make a great partner or friend. This is the halo effect, which is the tendency we have to attribute positive qualities to someone because we like a certain personality trait, or we like their sense of humor or their generosity, and so on, or because we seem to have similar views and/or tastes.

For example, when we see a beautiful celebrity, we may automatically assume that this person is fun and loyal but this may be utterly inaccurate.

We are social primates and social interactions are in our nature, because they help us develop. We usually want to meet people, and we like to listen to and tell people stories. This way, we receive stimuli that affect our way of thinking and acting. We also tend to relate to various personas, and we eventually get to realize that no one is perfect and perfection lies in appreciating what is already there.

Therefore, it is of paramount importance to understand how you perceive other people and whether you are biased or not. We need to get to know other people deeply and we can only do this if we are truly interested in getting to know them. When we get to know others, we find out how to approach them and treat them well in order to make both them and ourselves happy.

When we get to know our family and our significant other and their communication style, we are able to communicate more effectively and avoid arguments. It is the same with friends and colleagues. When we truly know them, we know whether we can trust them with some or all of our thoughts and secrets and we know what to expect from them.

Be open and sincere and remember that your positive attitude will attract positive people who will help you learn and develop further. Smile and make someone else's day bright! Ultimately, it is love and kindness we all look for.

5.3 Trust

Most of us, if not all of us, have had our feelings hurt at least once in our life. Someone did not treat us right and they broke our trust. A friend, a girlfriend, a boyfriend, a spouse, a sibling, a parent, a colleague, a teacher, anyone who was once close to our heart might have betrayed us. However, trust is the foundation of every successful relationship, and a powerful tool. We all have the need to trust and be trusted. When people trust you, you can have a positive impact on them, and vice versa. Both will seek each other's advice and will have each other's back. Give trust and it shall be given unto you.

We briefly talked about building trust in the previous chapter so it is time to elaborate further. Building trust in a workplace and any other relationship is not that different. We just need to put a bit more effort into relationships and keep in mind that trust is earned gradually so we need to be patient. In order to build trust with your fellow people, just follow the tips below.

1. Be yourself. Stop caring about what others think and just be honest and tell the truth. Show everyone your real self so they can appreciate and/or like you for who you really are. Nobody is perfect so if you pretend to be something you are not, someone will sooner or later notice it. Therefore, next time you do not know or understand something, ask for help and clarifications.

2. Be open. Talk about your needs, worries, and ambitions. Tell people what bugs you. Express your feelings in a calm and positive way. Be transparent and explain your thought process, intentions, and rational arguments. Remember that we all think differently so you need to clearly communicate your concerns and never let people guess what is on your mind. Respectively listen to other

people; their needs and dreams and everything they want to share. Do not assume, do not interrupt, and do not get biased conclusions.

3. Be kind. Do not hurt people and do not lie to them. Respect, help, and encourage those surrounding you with no expectations. Share your knowledge, learn from others, improve, improvise, and adapt. Use "please" and "thank you," be on time, be friendly, and make them smile. Always focus on their positive qualities and appreciate them for who they are and what they emotionally offer you when they are in your life.

4. Be reliable. Be a person of your word and keep your promises. If you cannot follow through with your commitments, let people know in advance. Deliver what you promise. Do not compromise by doing something that comes against your values just to earn something and never tell people what they want to hear if you do not sincerely believe it because you will eventually lose your credibility.

5. Be respectful and assume responsibility. Arguments are normal in almost any social interaction that is frequent and lasts a few hours every day. Make sure that you always keep your self-control and respect others. Try to deescalate as quickly as possible. Everyone makes mistakes so do not try to pretend that you never make any. This will only make you lose your trustworthiness. On the contrary, admitting your mistakes will help you fix them.

6. Be clear about your boundaries. Setting boundaries is of paramount importance for your own physical and mental health. It means that you assume responsibility for your actions and feelings and others should do so for their

own. If you cannot do something that someone is asking you, just refuse so people understand what they can expect from you. For example, I do not like talking on the phone and the people around me are aware of this. Instead, I prefer texting. If someone calls me 12 times in a row, I will not pick up, and this should not come as a surprise to them. If it is an emergency, they will send me a text message and I will call them immediately.

In order to build trust in your serious romantic relationship, you need to make your relationship your number one priority. Talk about the future, make plans using words like "we" and "our" instead of "I" and "my," give your undivided attention and affection, and respect each other's boundaries. Be kind to each other, encourage each other, and never lie or betray your partner's trust.

If, however, your trust is broken but you want to work on it together and rebuild it, know that it will take time, over which you will feel weak and doubt your partner. If your partner cheated on you, or did something else that broke your trust, you need to be willing to work hard and believe them next time they go missing in action for five hours, for example. Are you able to do this? Some people are, but some people are not and doubts may break them.

5.4 Negative Emotions

Emotions are biological states associated with thoughts, feelings, behavioral responses, and pleasure or discontent. Paul Ekman, a psychologist and professor at the University of California, classified the core emotions and suggested six positive and negative core emotions.[16] The core emotions include anger, disgust, fear, happiness, surprise, and sadness.

Ekman's further research proposed other negative emotions including embarrassment, guilt, shame, despair, and jealousy.[17]

All emotions are normal and even negative emotions are useful if we properly respond to them. We are encouraged to focus on positivity but we need to understand that negative emotions are absolutely normal. All emotions are also contagious. Emotional contagion is the phenomenon of experiencing someone else's emotions and responding behaviors, so we need to take good care of ourselves and experience negative emotions only because we have responded to a genuine stimulus, and not because we have contracted it. We can also consciously try and transmit positive emotions to people feeling negative emotions, because negative emotions may have a huge impact on our health and wellness.

Keep in mind that if we poorly manage negative emotions and we stick to them, our stress hormone, cortisol, increases and we may experience health problems and/or insomnia. Just contemplate for a minute about the fact that Sigmund Freud labeled depression as "anger turned inward."[18] Learn how to empathize with others but always empathize with yourself first and practice self-care.

There are a number of factors causing negative emotions, such as a triggering event or our negative thoughts about an event or a situation. For example, we are sad after a breakup, we are angry when someone has treated us unfairly, we feel guilty if we have hurt someone, and so on. However, negative emotions can benefit us if we respond well because oftentimes they motivate us to take action both on a personal level if it is on a small scale and on a national or global level if it is on a large scale. Think about strikes and demonstrations around the world motivated by anger.

If we feel anxiety or anger, we try different things in order to stop experiencing these emotions, and this in turn leads to innovative solutions to our problems, so negative emotions can be motivating. Jealousy can also motivate us to improve and try harder so we get what other people get, provided that this will make us happy. Feeling guilt, on the other hand, makes us reflect on our actions and learn our lesson so we do not repeat the same mistake in the future. In order to be able to respond positively to negative emotions, we need to take a break when our head is filled up with them. If we take a break and fill up with positive experiences, we will have the required time to reflect and understand why we feel the way we feel and what we should really do about it.

So if you have not learnt to accept your negative emotions, now you know that you should always welcome them. It is easy to accept them. It will just take some practice from your side. Find the emotion and understand what it is, where it is coming from, and what makes you feel. If you are a visual person, use a pen and paper and make notes.

Once you identify your negative emotion, distance yourself and observe it as if it was an object. Describe its size, shape, and color, and whether it is moving or making a sound. This way, you know and accept that the emotion is real and eats you up internally. Keep in mind that you should keep your focus on the things that you can do and not on the things you cannot do. This is the way to address your negative emotion properly.

5.4.1 Dealing with Negative Emotions

I realize that with the current global crisis that most of us face for the first—and hopefully last—time, people need psychological and emotional support more than ever. It is not only our physical health at stake, but also our mental wellbeing.

COVID-19 has made many people feel like prisoners. All these people somehow need to vent their frustration. Therefore, managing negative emotions for those who have already acknowledged them is very important.

Remember that you first need to accept your emotions. Do not ignore your negative emotions. Do not pretend that they do not exist or affect you. Lying to yourself may temporarily feel good. In the long run, however, if you choose to ignore your negative emotion, it will fire back even stronger. When this happens, you may also experience physical symptoms such as headaches, stomach issues, insomnia, and autoimmune disorders, among others. You may escape having COVID-19, but you certainly do not want to have other symptoms.

As a rule of thumb, I have created the abbreviation **DAWN™** to help you.

Distance yourself from the emotion by taking a break.

Approach as if it is someone else's emotion. How would you advise them to handle it?

Work on an action plan to change everything you can change.

Nurse yourself by practicing self-care.

Once you have accepted your negative emotions, you can then deal with them. You can use the following steps for the most effective management of your negative emotions.

1. Understand your emotion.

How do you feel? How has it affected you and your life? What is the cause of this emotion? Remember that it is fine to feel weak at times. You know this emotion will finally cease and you will fix yourself as soon as it passes.

2. Take a break from your emotion.

Stop mulling it over for a while and relax. Read, dance, meditate, exercise, talk to a loved one, laugh, or do anything that will take your mind off the specific situation. If nothing works, try to count from one to ten, as it sometimes works miracles!

3. Distance yourself.

Observe as if you were watching a movie or reading a book. What would you advise Harry Potter, Frodo, Ethan Hunt, Hermione Granger, Wonder Woman, or Miss America to do if they felt the same way?

4. Act on your emotion.

Find the positives in this negative situation and do what you can do. Change and learn so you can guard yourself better next time. Remember that there is always a positive. For example, during a COVID-19 lockdown, it may be that you get to spend quality time with your family or you get to learn something new, or you get to clean your house thoroughly, or a million other things you find interesting, fun, or relaxing.

If you feel anger and your blood is boiling, instead of shouting, distance yourself and identify the reason behind your anger. Did someone do something they should not have done according to your beliefs or values? If you are in a context where you can explain this to the other person (work, relationship) just explain to them that this is very important to you and it upsets you. If you are in a context where you will never encounter this person again (road rage, bank, public service), distance yourself and realize that if you become angry, you allow the other person to control you and this is not something you want. Do you want to make this person strong and allow them to have such an impact on you? No!

If you feel disgusted by something unpleasant or offensive, distance yourself and identify the reason why. Is it something against your moral compass? Again, if you can, talk to the person calmly and explain your thought process. Otherwise, do not allow the other person to control how you feel.

If you feel fear, assess the situation objectively. Is there a dangerous situation or a potential failure? If yes, believe in yourself and make a plan for how you will proceed and tackle the situation. Recall past experiences and fill up with energy from past success. Now channel all this positivity to your new plan.

Finally, if you feel sadness, you need to identify who or what is behind it. If it is you because you are not satisfied with an outcome at work, for example, motivate yourself and improve so you can succeed in the future. If you think someone else is behind it, assess whether you have managed your expectations as you should have and learn the lesson life is offering. If you feel grief, which is a completely different emotion, remember it will eventually pass and no emotion lasts forever. Have you lost your job? Identify how you can become competitive and look for a job where you will not be expendable.

5.4.2 Managing Negative Emotions at Work

We can spend many hours of our day at work and our job makes us feel an abundance of emotions. We can feel happy and accomplished when we reach a goal, but we can also feel angry and frustrated if things do not go as planned or if our boss treats us terribly. We can also feel intimidated if someone is bullying us. When we are in the workplace, we need to keep our temper and control our reactions because we cannot start shouting, venting, or crying in front of others. All these may make perfect sense at the time, but they may be perceived as signs of weakness by others at the workplace.

If you feel negative emotions filling you up, take a break, breathe deeply, count to 10, and leave the office for a few minutes. Go for a walk, call a loved one, browse funny videos, cry it off in a private place, or do something that will take your mind off it. If the negative emotion is repeated every day, for example if you are bullied or harassed, make sure you talk to someone in the Human Resources department, if there is one, and recommend a course of action. If there is no resolution, start looking for another job.

Keep in mind that you should never take decisions when you are emotional because chances are you will later regret them. Make sure you have not misunderstood something or something has not been miscommunicated, and do not let your negative emotions cloud your judgment. Take a decision after you have calmed down and identified the exact issue, and only if you have exhausted possible solutions.

When I worked for a company, my boss quit and I knew that the person who would take over was a person bullying his subordinates and badmouthing the upper management. That person was one of the investors in the company so the upper management could not do anything but stand him. I had to quit. Two other heads quit because of the same guy. It is a sign of strength to quit, because you realize that the circumstances do not serve you. You realize you need something better for yourself, and you go after it.

If you are jealous of or admire a colleague because they always reach their goals, get promoted, and clients seem to love them, approach them openly and identify how you can improve and what you can learn from this person. Make sure your jealousy is not turned to envy and never gossip them. Motivate yourself with their victories and show the proper respect.

Remember that you should treat others the way you want to be treated.

If you feel resentment because your efforts and value are not recognized, or because they always make you work overtime without getting additional payment or a promotion, or because you are not given the opportunity to develop personally and professionally, talk to your boss and explain to them that you have lost your motivation. If they do not resolve it, start looking for another job.

We are only humans and we may occasionally lose control. No matter how well we have prepared, unexpected events may cause us to go off the rails and behave in an inappropriate way. If this is the case, admit you were wrong for reacting the way you did, and apologize for your outburst.

A tip I always follow, and it has been serving me well, is to not bring my home problems to work and vice versa. If your home problems follow you to work, focus on your work goals and action plans. If your work is following you home, find a way that will help you release negativity, such as hitting the gym or playing a game, or anything else that suits your interests.

5.4.3 Managing Negative Emotions in Relationships

When we spend a lot of time with someone, negative emotions are sometimes unavoidable. Consider that we sometimes argue with our self, let alone another person! What you should do is to focus on the positives every time an issue arises and view challenges as opportunities so that you can keep a positive outlook and attitude.

When you quarrel, stop blaming the other person and assume your part of the responsibility. It is rarely only one's fault. We all make mistakes so it is not a sign of weakness to admit your own mistakes. Just make sure you learn from them and never repeat them.

Laugh with your partner. Laughter brings us closer and it is a great positive way to release negative emotions, such as anxiety and sadness. Couples who laugh together get to know, bond, support, and encourage each other more.

Always remember that the way you respond to a negative emotion or a tough situation can be entirely different to the way your significant other responds. This does not mean that something has gone wrong with one of you, it just means that you have developed different coping mechanisms and one of you may need more time, so be there and support them.

5.5 Conclusion

What is happiness? I would guess that you have wondered and pondered about this question before reading this book. You may have an answer that applies to you personally. If this is the case, this is wonderful. It means you know how to be happy and work with your happiness as the end goal.

People reaching self-actualization, therefore their happiness, hold strong views and fight for them no matter what others may think or say. Even though sense of belonging and appreciation are lower in the hierarchy of needs, someone may persist and skip these needs when they are true to themselves and reach self-actualization. They do not care if someone disrespects them, and this is absolutely fine. They know who they are and they do not need to prove anything to anyone.

Thomas Edison tried for years and failed again and again before he invented the first incandescent light bulb. His haters thought he was a weird man wasting time. However, Edison made it and when asked about his failed attempts, he apparently said "I have not failed. I've just found 10,000 ways that [light bulbs] won't work."[19] Who does not know the name Edison? Does anyone know his haters' names? No!

As a matter of fact, a pattern is observed among those who have managed to reach the top of the happiness pyramid. These people have increased self-awareness, accept and appreciate everyone with their positives and negatives, are independent and creative, see things objectively, are not easily deceived, are often unconventional and they do not necessarily follow norms. They are usually very private people who need alone time, they are kind, moral, and fun to be around with a close social circle and they are not interested in shallow relationships. They care about humanity and they are happy with who they are, and do not expect other people's approval. They also, often, feel spiritually elevated or deeply connected with nature. Therefore, as long as you stay true to yourself, fear nobody's judgment and pursue your happiness without worrying about your image and how others perceive you.

5.6 Assignment for Reflection

Read the following statements and write what emotion(s) Dalin is experiencing. How would you advise Dalin to handle the situations and manage their negative emotions? The following list is not based on true facts.

When you complete the exercise, take under consideration that all these do not happen at the same time—not even in the same year.

a. "Dalin, you did not reach your sales goals this semester. Your colleague, Belak, did, so I have to promote her instead."

b. A driver missed the stop sign and hit Dalin's car. The car has moderate damage but no one was hurt.

c. "Dalin, you knew from the beginning that I play video games. You cannot ask me to stop doing something that pleases me because you do not like video games. The fact that we live together does not mean we have to spend every minute doing things together," said Dalin's romantic partner.

6 Vision Planning and Goals Setting

6.1 Vision Planning

Carl Jung, father of analytical psychology, said "Your vision will become clear only when you can look into your own heart. Who looks outside, dreams; who looks inside, awakes."[20]

While creating your vision may seem trivial and a waste of time, it is actually a lot more important than you can imagine. It is the map that leads to your success and happiness while you remain true to yourself and your opinions. It is what will hold you accountable against distractions and against other people's needs and wants. It is your success plan that will guide your life in every aspect, such as career, family, health, and friendship. For these reasons, you need to think, maybe for the very first time, what you **really** want instead of what you do not want. Now is the time to dream big.

Your vision statement will help you identify and visualize the life you really want and the actions you need to take in order to get there. It is your compass that will guide you to the right mindset, and this is why you need to take under consideration your values, skills, strengths, weaknesses, hobbies, things you enjoy, as well as what really matters to you, what makes you feel accomplished, your hopes, and your goals in every aspect of your life.

Before you start developing your vision statement, work on old and open wounds first. Hurtful memories are like open wounds. You cannot envision your ideal life if old wounds keep you stuck in the past. If you hurt, find a way to heal, and if people treated you badly, forgive them. This is the only way to move ahead.

Take as much time as you need in order to write your vision statement, and know that you can change it later as your priorities change. As we grow older, our statement may and can change. Describe how you imagine your ideal life in your vision statement, and make it as short or as long you find appropriate, but keep in mind that the more details you include, the better. Write in present tense because your vision comes to life as soon as you start working on it and visualizing it. Take your life in your hands now.

Once you write your vision statement, you can read it as often as you want. It can be at the beginning of each day or each week, or every time you feel lost and you cannot recall the purpose of your life. This is a way of self-care as it will stir you back to the right direction and it will remind you of every small or bigger victory so far.

6.2 Introduction to Neuro-Linguistic Programming (NLP)

NLP stands for neuro-linguistic programming and is the way we use the language to create our world and achieve our desired outcomes. It began as a model of communication with ourselves and others, and it was developed by Richard Bandler and John Grinder.[21] This model explains how we process information we gather through our senses. Usually, there is an external event that we process internally, and this internal process (representation) is then associated with an emotional state.

Neuro represents the nervous system (mind) and how we experience events through our five senses (sight, smell, sound, taste, touch).

Linguistic represents language and nonverbal communication through which our neural representations are coded and given meaning, and includes feelings and self-talk and words to/from others.

Programming is about the ability to identify and utilize the communication "software" we run in our neurological systems to achieve our desired outcomes.

NLP helps us change things in our internal representations consciously, and ultimately remodeling our world with our desired outcomes. For this reason, we need to focus on what we want so that we can fill up with positive thoughts, which in turn generate positive feelings, bringing us to a positive state.

6.3 Goals Setting with the Assistance of NLP

Now that you have developed your vision statement, you need to start breaking it into long-term and short-term goals, and breaking these goals further into tasks. In order to create goals properly, they need to be SMART. SMART stands for Specific, Measurable, Achievable, Realistic, and Time-based. You need to use this format because you will then be able to measure against your success and achievements.

An easy breakdown structure you can use for breaking down your vision statement to smaller, more manageable tasks is the following:

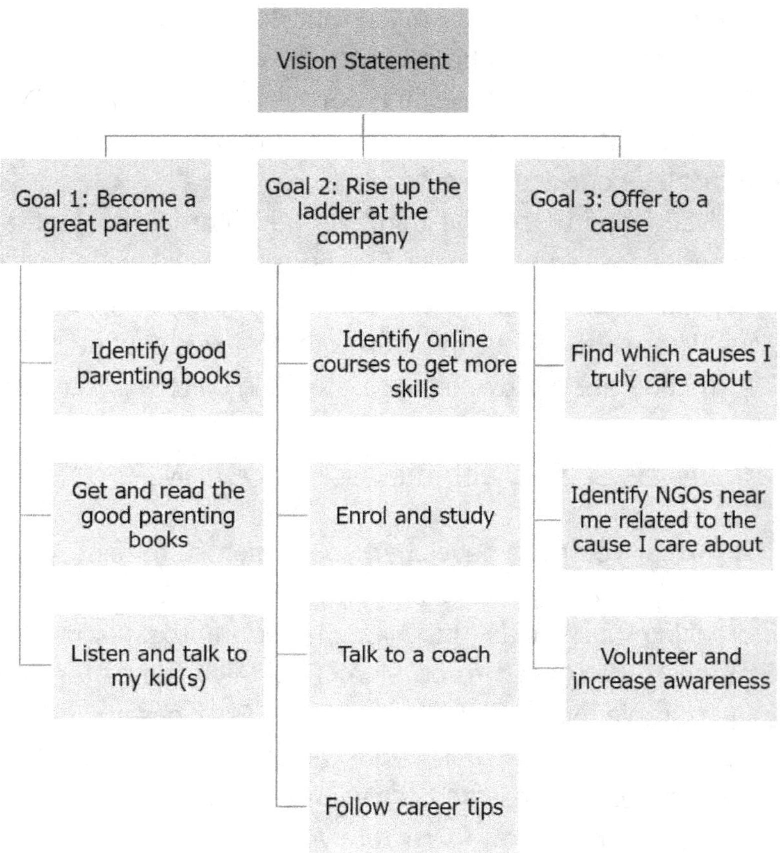

Goals will motivate you and will help you identify the steps you have to take in order to achieve them. Once you start reaching your goals, you will be proud of yourself and self-confident so you will need to celebrate your victories! Even if you fail, remember that there is no failure. There is only feedback that helps us improve, or feedback that asks us to reassess our goal.

Create goals for everything that matters to you, such as family, relationships, career, finance, education, arts, hobbies, and anything you deem important. Once you have goals for all the important aspects of your life, break them into smaller tasks that will lead you to the achievement of your goals. For example, if your goal is to change career in three years, identify what courses you need to attend and start studying.

Remember to write realistic goals with as many details as possible, and always focus on DOs instead of DON'Ts. Look at the wheel of life in Chapter 8, and identify the areas that you want to work on. The following questions will also help you turn your focus from a current state to the desired state so you can develop appropriate goals.

1. What is the current state that you want to change?
2. What do you want to stop or avoid?
3. Who has already achieved your desired state, and how would you describe them?
4. Which qualities, associated with your desired state, do you already have that you would like to have more of? Which ones do you not have and would like to develop?
5. Imagine you have achieved your goal. What would you be doing or doing more of?

In order to create goals with achievable outcomes, you need to transform from a goal setter to a goal getter. The following tips will help you achieve your outcomes and write your goals properly.

1. **State it in positive**: What exactly do you want? Where, when, how, and with whom do you want it?
2. **Specify your current situation**: Where are you now regarding your desired outcome?
3. **Envision the desired outcome**: Imagine as if you have achieved your goal. What do you see, hear, touch, and feel? Make it compelling.
4. **Specify your test process**: How will you know when you have achieved your desired outcome?

5. **Focus on what this outcome will allow you to do**: Does it affect only you or other people as well? In which ways?
6. **Identify the required resources**: What do you already have? What else do you need in order to achieve your goal?
7. **Reflect on the past**: Have you ever had or done this before? How did you feel?
8. **Confirm that the outcome is moral**: What will or will not happen if you get it?

Now you are ready to set your goals! Remember that when you achieve a goal, you should celebrate it. Notice your progress, and reward yourself so you can build up the self-confidence you deserve.

6.4 Eliminating Limiting Beliefs with NLP

Do you remember when we talked about the Attributional Retraining in the first chapter of this book? Attributional Retraining enhances performance because individuals' negative beliefs are replaced by positive and helpful thoughts sustaining motivation. NLP can assist you in reprogramming your mind and getting rid of your limiting beliefs, so that achieving your goals becomes easier.

A limiting belief is something that stops you from being the person you want to be. Limiting beliefs are like open wounds that keep you stuck and frustrated. If for example you believe that you cannot stop procrastinating or you cannot get things organized, then you have to attend to this limiting belief and overcome it.

I want you to get rid of your limiting beliefs, and this is why I have created the following script so you can use it at home. It is difficult to read and work on yourself at the same time, so you may either learn it by heart, or record yourself on your phone, and then relax and listen to your own voice guiding you during the limiting belief elimination process. The optimal choice is, however, to ask a trusted person to help you as it is helpful to keep notes, and it is best to keep your eyes closed during the process so that you can visualize images better.

<u>Limiting Belief Elimination Script</u>

"Close your eyes. Can you think of a limiting belief about yourself that you wish you did not have? What is it? ... As you think about it, can you picture it in your head? Visualize it and take a picture of what you see.

Make sure you spot the location, and catch any visual cues, such as whether it is black and white or colored, bright or dim, focused or defocused, a movie (as in a gif) or still, flat, or 3D. Then catch any auditory and kinesthetic cues. Are there any sounds? If yes, can you identify them, their direction, volume, tempo, and duration? Are there any moving elements? Are you moving in the frame?

There is at least one feeling that is important. Maybe there are more feelings. Please focus on how you feel and name the feeling or feelings.

Can you think of a belief that is no longer true.22 For example, someone might have been a heavy drinker in the past. Back then, they used to believe they were a heavy drinker but they have stopped drinking since, and they no longer believe that. Or when you believed you were 10 years old when you were actually 10 years old, but now you no longer are. Do you have something like that which used to be true for you, but no longer is? ... Good, what is it?

As you think about that old belief, can you picture it in your head? Visualize it and take a picture of what you see. Make sure you spot the location and catch any visual cues, such as whether it is black and white or colored, bright or dim, focused or defocused, a movie (as in a gif) or still, flat, or 3D. Then catch any auditory and kinesthetic cues. Are there any sounds? If yes, can you identify them, their direction, volume, tempo, and duration? Are there any moving elements? Are you moving in the frame?"

You have now completed the first part of this process and you need to compare your answers (from the two pictures) and match them across. Matching across transfers the elements from a particular state to another, and changes your internal representations from a particular event to another. This creates a positive state.

In other words, now that you have documented the elements associated with your internal representation of a current limiting belief and an old belief, you have to change your internal representation for your limiting belief according to your internal representation of your old belief.

For example, your current limiting belief is that you cannot lose weight, and you see a black and white, zoomed in, dim, and 3D movie while you listen to classical music. Your old belief is that you were a 16-year-old teenager and you see a still image, full of colors, sounds of pop music, and lots of balloons surrounding you. You need to insert the image of your limiting belief in the image of your old belief. This will result in you seeing an image full of colors, sounds of pop music, and yourself surrounded by balloons while you become slim.

Once you have managed to do this, you need to proceed to the second part of the process, and test yourself by asking what you think about your old belief (of being unable to lose weight).

"Can you think of a belief that for you is absolutely true? Like for example the belief that oceans are full of water. Do you believe that? ... Good, what is it? As you think about that belief, can you imagine it in your head? Visualize it and take a screenshot of what you see. Make sure you spot the location and catch any visual cues, such as whether it is black and white or colored, bright or dim, focused or defocused, a movie (as in a gif) or still, flat, or 3D. Then catch any auditory and kinesthetic cues. Are there any sounds? If yes, can you identify them, their direction, volume, tempo, and duration? Are there any moving elements? Are you moving in the frame?

Can you think of a new, empowering belief that you want to have, which is the opposite of the old limiting belief? ... Good, what is it? As you think about that belief, can you imagine it in your head? Visualize it and take a screenshot of what you see. Make sure you spot the location and catch any visual cues, such as whether it is black and white or colored, bright or dim, focused or defocused, a movie (as in a gif) or still, flat, or 3D. Then catch any auditory and kinesthetic cues. Are there any sounds? If yes, can you identify them, their direction, volume, tempo and duration? Are there any moving elements? Are you moving in the frame?"

Now that you have completed these steps, you need to compare your answers and match, as described above, so that you change the internal representation for your limiting belief, and see the image of the limiting belief with all of the elements of the image of your strong belief that is absolutely true to you.

Once you have matched across, test yourself by asking what you believe now. Clap your hands in front of your face so you can seal in your new belief and enjoy!

Use the following table to keep notes over all the four images. Just mark each field that is associated with each image.

Cues V (Visual) A (Auditory) K (Kinesthetic)	Image of limiting belief	Image of old belief	Image of absolutely true belief	Image of new belief
V: Bright or dim?				
V: Black and white or colored?				
V: Focused or defocused?				
V: A movie or still?				
V: Flat or 3D?				
A: Are there any sounds? Can you identify them?				
A: What is the direction of the sound?				
A: Loud or low?				
A: Fast or slow?				

A: Instant or continuous?				
K: Are there any moving elements? Can you identify them?				
K: Can you describe the moving elements?				
K: Are you moving in the frame?				

6.5. Reprograming Our Unconscious with NLP

There are a few NLP techniques in order to help people wishing to change and reprogram their mind. In this section, there are two ways presented so you can try on your own. Remember that language allows us to process, interpret, and communicate our internal thoughts, and also reshape our world and entire life.

6.5.1. Loomie Technique

The Loomie technique is used for changing or overcoming minor negative behaviors that are hard to let go, such as nail-biting, smoking, and more. The change is usually instant and impressive. Loomie helps us make new choices instead of removing habits. This means that instead of stopping a behavior, we replace this behavior with one that serves us.

Before you proceed with the script, keep in mind that you need to be fully associated in the old image. This means that you will be part of the image. In the final image, however, you are dissociated, that is you look at the image from afar. In all the images, be very precise about the details. Speed is of paramount importance so you need to speak really fast. A tip to follow is to have breaks between each Loomie technique, and remember to close your eyes during each step of the process, and open them again between each step.

<u>Loomie Technique Script & Instructions</u>

Focus and visualize what represents the habit or situation you would like to change. Associate and look through your own eyes. Identify cues just like described in the previous exercise.

"Close your eyes. Is it alright with your unconscious mind for you to make this change today, and for you to be aware of it consciously? How do you know it's time to _______? (e.g., bite your nails). Identify the trigger. When you think of _____________________ (the negative behavior you want to change), can you visualize it? ... Picture it, and make it so you are looking through your eyes. This is your old image. Seal in the image by snapping your fingers. Clear the screen and open your eyes. Think of something entirely different."

Focus and visualize the person you would like to be and the alternative behavior you would like to have instead. Associate and look through your own eyes.

"What would you like to do instead? Close your eyes. When you think of this ________ (alternative behavior), can you visualize it? Picture it, and make it so you are looking through your eyes. Make the image as compelling as possible. If you made it brighter, more colorful, with music would it be more compelling? If yes, make it as you want. If not, leave it as it is. Increase the positive feelings as much as possible... Good, now step out of the image so you can see your body in it. This is now your new image. Seal it in by snapping your fingers. Clear the screen and open your eyes. Think of something entirely different."

Bring back the old image, insert the new image, dissociated, into the lower left-hand corner, small and dark. At the same time, take the old image, shrink it very fast, and look at it from afar, while the new dark image explodes into full screen, big and bright. You can internally or externally make a "loomie" sound but it is not necessary. However, it is very important that this process takes place very, very quickly.

"Close your eyes. Now, can you take the old image and bring it up on the screen? Make sure that you are looking through your eyes... Good, as you have the old image on the screen, can you see the new image in the lower left-hand corner, small and dark? Make sure you see yourself in the image. In a moment, I want you to have the new image explode big and bright and have it explode up so that it covers the old image, while the old image shrinks down and becomes small and dark in the lower left-hand corner. Do this as quickly as I say 'loomie' ... OK. One, two, three, loomie. Now, clear the screen. Open your eyes... Close your eyes."

Repeat the last step at least five times and when you get to the new positive image, hold it for a few seconds so you can really enjoy it. Repeat more times if necessary, until you can no longer recall the old image. Once you can no longer recall the old image, test yourself by visualizing the future.

"Try to bring the old image back. You may find that you cannot."

If you can still see the negative image, repeat the last step a few more times until you can no longer see it.

That was the Loomie technique so you can adopt a positive alternative to a negative behavior. Old image, new image, one, two, three, loomie, clear the screen! Keep in mind that you have to do this very fast and you are not allowed to slow down during the process.

6.5.2 Parts Reconciliation

The next technique is called Parts Reconciliation and unlike the Loomie technique, there is no need for speed, and you can take your time during the process. It is used to resolve internal conflict, creating peace between parts of the unconscious mind, so that all parts are aligned. You can use it when you are torn between two opposing beliefs, and want to feel empowered. For example, a part of you may believe you deserve success while another part of you may believe you do not. Use this technique so your unconscious mind parts align that you deserve success, happiness, and everything else you want!

Parts Reconciliation Script & Instructions

First, identify the problem and the conflicting parts. Ask your unconscious mind to identify which part is the unwanted part.

Whatever comes first to your mind is the correct answer. Then, sit and set up your arms out in front and parallel with your palms face up. Ensure that your arms are not sitting anywhere and can come easily together and start reading (or have someone else read) the following script.

"I would like to invite the part of you that believes ___________ (the unwanted part), to come out and stand on either the left or the right hand. Which hand would it like to stand on?"

At this point you have named either your right or left hand with the unwanted part.

"Create the image of the unwanted part with as many details as possible. Does that remind you of anyone you know? What are they wearing? Are they saying anything? Are there any feelings attached to the image? Answer and thank this part."

Now bring up the opposite part.

"I'd like to talk to the part with which this part is most in conflict, the wanted part that believes ___________ (the wanted part) and let's have it come out and stand on the other hand. Would it like to stand on the front, middle, or back of that hand? Create the image of the wanted part with as many details as possible. Does that remind you of anyone you know? What are they wearing? Are they saying anything? Are there any feelings attached to the image? Answer and thank this part."

Separate your intention from your behavior and understand the parts. Start with the unwanted part.

> "Close your eyes. I would like to talk to the unwanted part, the part that believes _________ standing on your left/right hand (the one you named earlier). For what purpose does it hold that belief? For what purpose is it there? What does it serve you or not with? What is its intention?"

Keep asking these questions and chunk them up (move from specific, or small-scale ideas or pieces of information to more general, larger ones) until the hand with the unwanted part moves toward the other hand. Remember the word that caused the move while you remain associated. What do these things give you? What is the purpose of all these things? When your hand moves, tell it to yourself.

> "Your _____ hand just moved toward the other hand. You did not do that consciously, did you? Thank this part."

Chunk up the wanted part until you get to the same or a similar word that caused the movement for the unwanted part (by repeating the understanding your intention and behavior step you just completed for the wanted part this time). As the hands begin to move together say:

> "Notice that both parts have the same ultimate intention of ____________. Notice that both parts were once part of a larger whole and can become whole again through the process of integration. Ask each part to look across and notice the resources that the other part has and to consider the possibility of sharing those resources and working

together in synergy and harmony to achieve the ultimate intention of _____________."

Repeat this step until your hands touch. When your hands touch, gently move them to your chest.

"Bring these parts inside and allow them to become whole again at the unconscious level, right now."

Stay in silence for 30 seconds.

"In your own time, come back into the room."

6.6. Conclusion

According to the Project Management Institute, "a project is a temporary endeavor to create a unique product, service or result."[23] So rather much anything that currently exists only in your imagination is a potential project. The food you will cook, the song or the story you want to write, the ideal career you want to pursue, or a gold medal in the Olympics.

The common base of all the above things is that they entail a beginning, an executed plan, and an ending. Even for the smallest project you can imagine, such as boiling an egg, there is already a plan in your head. You will take a pot, you will pour some water and place the egg, and you will let it boil for a few minutes. The more details we include in a plan, the easier its management and monitoring become.

What I would like you to remember from this chapter is that when we identify the core of our issues and explain it with as many details as possible, it is easier to resolve them.

6.7 Assignment for Reflection

Write your vision statement and break it down to at least two long-term goals and several short-term tasks.

7 Obstacles and How to Overcome Them

Like many people, you may have dreams and you may set various goals. By reading this far, you have probably learnt a lot about yourself, about who you want to be, and what the purpose of your life is. You are willing to work hard, you have even started the work required to make your dreams come true. And then, you run into roadblocks. What are you supposed to do when obstacles pop up in your way? Panic? Give up? NO! Certainly not.

If success was easy, everyone would be an achiever. You have your vision statement worked out, and you have set your SMART goals. But what will you do when you find roadblocks? Of course, you will overcome them.

The way you perceive obstacles is the way you will overcome them too. If you see them as puzzles where you need to put the pieces together, then you will look at them as works of art and opportunities to learn from. On the other hand, if you see them as a threat that will not allow you to succeed, you will not be able to respond appropriately because you will fill up with negativity and may give up altogether.

There is no single achiever who has not met at least one obstacle on their way to success or happiness. It is an expected part of the process and while obstacles can sometimes be easily overcome, there are other times when there is nothing to be done and the achiever needs to find a way around them.

Next time you deal with an obstacle and get discouraged, remember that Edgar Allan Poe suffered from depression and alcohol and drug abuse, Helen Keller was deaf and blind, Ludwig Van Beethoven was deaf, Martin Luther King Jr. was arrested and sent to jail, John Nash was schizophrenic, and Walt Disney was dyslexic and had attention deficit disorder. These are just some famous people who battled their obstacles and offered us a lot of inspiration through their achievements.

7.1 Types of Obstacles

There are two types of obstacles: internal and external. Internal obstacles generally come from our subconscious mind, such as fear and anger, but they can also be personality traits, such as procrastination and lack of discipline. External obstacles are outside of our control, such as the economy, wars, pandemics, and natural disasters. However, even if they are outside our control, we need to remain focused on our target and deal with them as best as we can.

7.2 Challenges Our Subconscious Mind Sets

Do you remember when you tried to ride a bicycle for the first time or drive a car? Or cook dinner or even try to swallow a pill? First attempts are usually difficult. However, the more you practice, the easier it gets and less conscious awareness is required. At some points, it even starts happening automatically and naturally. This automatic mechanism is executed by the subconscious mind.

The biggest part of our behavior is driven by our subconscious mind, just like our reflexes. Our subconscious mind lists some things as "ok" and some others as "not ok" for us, and these listed items are based on past positive and negative experiences. When we have a negative experience, we want to forget about it as well as all the negative emotions associated with it, and we usually end up consciously forgetting it. However, our subconscious mind has it stored. These negative memories that are subconsciously stored are our subconscious pain points. When we experience a new event that subconsciously triggers these pain points, we usually respond poorly and we may lose our self-control.

The most common internal obstacles that deal with these subconscious pain points are fear and perfectionism.

7.2.1 Fear

Fear can make you reluctant to start anything new because it fills you up with doubts and worries about a potential failure. Sometimes, you may be thinking of your potential embarrassment in case things do not work out. Fear derives from our ancient instinct of self-preservation and it visits us when we are unsure about our future and what it holds. Will we be able to have a secure job that will provide us with money to pay our bills and food to eat? Will we have people around us who will care about us?

Fear is never productive so remember what Martin Luther King said: "Fear knocked at the door, faith answered, there was no one there."[24] The only thing to be afraid of is the actual fear. Once you face your fear, you will see there is nothing there. Live in the present, focus on what you have, identify your strengths, believe in yourself, and work hard. Use your positive thinking and positive attitude deriving from your growth mindset, do not magnify trivial issues, and do not play scenarios in your mind starting with "what if."

7.2.2 Perfectionism

Do you want everything to be perfect so that you can grade it with an A+? Well, you need to come back to reality. Absolutely nothing in nature is perfect. Perfectionism is a beautiful lie conceived by story tellers for literature, poetry, theater, and cinema.

Do not wait for the perfect timing for anything in your life, simply because this will most likely never come. Finding obstacles in your way is natural, and it will almost always happen, so stand up and begin to overcome them if you want to succeed.

Stop analyzing everything over and over again because you will only procrastinate and you may miss one or more good opportunities. Sure, you need a lot of information and details in order to take educated decisions that will have a great impact, but if you have reached a level where no more information is available, you have to decide and act right now.

If you struggle with taking decisions, the underlying cause may be perfectionism. If we chunk down perfectionism, we may locate low self-confidence that needs to be addressed. If your low self-confidence makes you hesitant about taking decisions, it is because you are never sure you know what is right for you. Trust me, deep down, you know what is right for you. You just need to have faith in yourself and trust your judgment that you will take the right decision. If I trust you that you can take the best decision, how can you not trust yourself?

7.2.3 Inner Conflict

When we perceive life as unfair, we feel anger and frustration, and even though it is normal to feel like this from time to time, if we stick to this belief, we will remain angry and frustrated. This, in turn, may harm our mental and physical health, which may have an impact on our personal relationships.

Stop comparing yourself to others, and do not feel inferior or unlucky. This will only demotivate you. Believe in your abilities and work hard. If others try to damage your self-confidence, just ignore them. You will always have haters when you are great at what you do. People who don't have a purpose in life often dislike successful people, because they remind them of what they could do and have if they actually worked hard. Haters are lazy and lack motivation so they cannot accept that you have been working hard.

Haters are basically jealous. They are negative people who can only feel joy when they diminish, humiliate, and make other people suffer. They cannot feel happiness any other way. As soon as you accept this, everything will be easier.

No matter what you do, there will always be people complaining and venting. It does not matter how much you wish you could help these people, they do not wish to be changed. Accept that they will never understand you and there is nothing you can do to change their mind and move ahead being fabulous.

7.3 Habits and Addictions

A habit is a routine behavior and it can be either positive or negative. A positive habit is brushing your teeth before you go to bed. A negative habit is like a minor addiction, for example, eating junk food often that may lead to poor health. We are creatures of habit because repetition creates familiarity, and we always feel good with a familiar pattern.

The difference between a habit and an addiction is the physical symptoms of withdrawal once someone acts and quits the addiction. If you are not sure whether you or someone you know have an addiction, ask the following questions:

1. Does it have a negative impact on your life?

2. Have you tried to hide it from people who care about you?
3. Have you been doing it more often as time goes by?
4. Do you feel nervous when you cannot do it?
5. Do you miss work or social activities because of it?

If you answered yes to most questions, then you need to understand there might be an addiction problem.

7.3.1 Addressing the Addiction

If you have an addiction, and you want to address it so it stops holding you back, this is great news. You have already acknowledged the problem, and this is half of its solution. Now, you may need to ask for help. Talk to a therapist or a doctor to see how you can proceed about it if you cannot make it on your own. Truth is, it is hard to quit with no outside help, but it is not always impossible.

Remember that focusing on a higher purpose will help your effort. Perhaps you could try to help other people overcome their addictions by joining a non-governmental organization, or find a cause you truly believe in, and do some community and charity work, so you keep your mind there. As we said earlier, our mind can focus on one thing at a time so if you focus on providing, you will defocus from your addiction.

You also need to understand that nobody will quit the addiction but you. A doctor, a therapist, or a coach can show you the way, and support you, but nothing will happen until you commit to do it yourself.

Many years ago, when I was 18, I volunteered at a local organization that helped drug addicts to quit. I remember this specific guy, Constantine, who was hospitalized after an overdose, for the third time. Two other people and I visited him at the hospital for moral support, and he started talking to us about how he does not want to quit. I still remember, 20 years later, that he would describe to us how excited he was every time he bought his drugs, and how much he liked preparing them for use. His father would try to help him, but he never decided to commit. I found out a few years later that Constantine had passed away due to an overdose.

7.4 Strategy on Overcoming Obstacles

Now that you know more about obstacles, it is time to roll up your sleeves and learn how to overcome them. You just need to follow the steps below.
1.   Distance yourself to understand the obstacle.
When an obstacle comes up, you may be very emotional so you need to take a break instead of reacting immediately. Your emotions are normal, but they should not hinder your success. Successful people bump to obstacles, so accept that this is part of the game. Distance yourself to identify the obstacle so you can then find out how to overcome it.

Think about what, who, where, why, when, and how. Is there anything you can do about it? Do you need someone else's help? Is it usually there? Did you do something to cause it? What do you know about it? Has anyone you know overcome it? What would you tell someone if they faced the same obstacle?
2.   Collect resources.
If you are not sure how to deal with the obstacle, ask people you trust for help and/or ideas. They may be able to direct you to solutions you have not thought of yet. We do not all have the same knowledge, experience, or expertise so ask around, look

it up online, and focus on your strengths and improvement in order to overcome the obstacle.

Manage your impatience and use time to your advantage. The harder the obstacle, the more time it will take to be overcome. You have the time to study and learn new skills, to find the right tools, or try and find the best process for your situation. Be flexible and open-minded. Try things and be creative.

3. Develop and execute your plan.

You may use a method that worked for a similar issue or you may find a new solution.

Create your time-based action plan, break it down to a list of tasks, prioritize them, and start working on them. When you work on smaller chunks of work, it is easier to see the patterns, tools, and techniques that will help you.

Be disciplined, focus on your goal, and do not give up. Successful people do not give up. They either overcome the obstacle or find a way around it. Have you heard of the Finnish concept "Sisu"? Sisu describes determination, and it means that you do not stop trying until you achieve your goal. This is the mentality and the way to go.

4. Lessons learnt.

After you have overcome the obstacle, take the time to assess and understand what the meaning of the obstacle was. What lessons did it teach you? Did it want you to change direction, and change something big in your life? Learn from failures and celebrate successes. Once you overcome your obstacle, reflect on what you did. Learn from any mistakes, and be well prepared for next time.

Over the course of this process, keep in mind that staying positive is the key to hack your subconscious mind. Focus on other areas of life that go well so you can remain strong.

Visualize overcoming your obstacle and achieving your goal, and treat the obstacle as an opportunity to learn and grow, always staying affirmative on your thoughts.

Remember that not all obstacles are overcome with our first attempt. Start over and execute as many plans that are required until you move ahead.

7.5 Conclusion

As you see, we may not realize it, but we are responsible for many obstacles in our way. Some of them are put there because of our thoughts and behaviors, some are there because we allow others to place them, and of course some other obstacles are outside our control. However, for the two first types of obstacles, the responsibility comes to us to clear the pathway and conquer success with confidence.

7.6 Assignment for Reflection

Reflect on how you look at challenges and obstacles up to now, and write down how you will look at them from now on. If you currently face an obstacle then write down your action plan now.

8 Self-Awareness & Coaching

8.1 What Self-Awareness Is

Self-awareness is the understanding of one's own personality, character, feelings, motives, desires, strengths, weaknesses, pros, cons, thoughts, beliefs, reactions, and attitude.

Results are generated through our actions. Our actions are generated through our beliefs, thoughts, emotions, interactions, and environment. All these are often unconscious and we do not pay attention to them. There are countless discussions in our heads and these usually lead our actions without even realizing it sometimes. The problem with all of this happening internally is that we do not consciously realize our limiting beliefs and flawed internal representations.

Sometimes, we may feel insecure, angry, or scared. If we take a break and introspect, we may realize that our response and reaction is part of something else, something bigger that has been triggered.

We should be open to learn about ourselves, because this is the way to identify and analyze what has happened, understand why we made the mistakes and choices we made, find solutions, and develop plans that will lead us to success and happiness.

One of the most touching statements I read while working on the results of the survey said "Thank you for reminding me how much I have." It seems that when someone reminds people what they already have, they remember to appreciate them and feel happier. In a broad sense, this is one of the things that coaching helps people with.

8.2 What Coaching Is

Coaching was developed in the 1980s when a special category of people emerged. These people were psychologically healthy but they needed guidance and support on a regular basis so they could achieve their goals and improve their lives.

Coaching is about finding the way from the person who you currently are to the person who you want to be in the future. It entails support, guidance, inspiration, and motivation in order to achieve personal and professional goals through personal development, learning, self-awareness, and accountability.

You already have all the answers inside you but you need to learn the way to access them. Some people choose to work with personal trainers to reach their fitness goals. Just like personal training, professional coaching is not the only way. You can self-coach to a great degree. It will just take longer to see results and, at times, you may doubt yourself because you lack the experience.

Coaching helps you create your own reality through your beliefs and internal representations and this is why accountability is significant. Coaching is about asking questions that beg for self-awareness and exploration of ways to achieve your dreams. Through inquiring, you will slowly realize you are empowered and accountable and you will understand that you can pursue what you want and become the person you want to be.

After the questioning and answering is done, coaching is about the development of action plans that you will need to work on so that you can achieve your goals. Coaching will push you out of your comfort zone and will ask you to make choices that may look impossible or scary. This way, your weaknesses will be reframed, and you will start to recognize your strengths.

At the end of the day, you will experiment, learn, and improve yourself and, therefore, your life.

Coaching works because the more you find out about yourself and what serves you or not, the better you identify what works for you in order to achieve success and happiness. When you recognize your weaknesses, you know how to work on them and improve your skills. On the other hand, when you recognize your strengths, you know how to do things more easily and you can find ways to overcome obstacles.

Coaching starts in the present and looks at the future. It helps you think outside the box and understand why you are stuck or why you have not achieved success and happiness and what you can do about it. Coaching brings tangible results because deep down you are fully capable of managing your negative emotions, such as anger or stress, finding the right balance between work and life, dealing with difficult life events, and eventually succeeding.

Coaching will help you with any or all of the following.

1. Goal setting: How to set goals in order to achieve success and happiness.
2. Understanding who you are: When you know who you are, you know how to improve.
3. Unleashing your potential: Identify and utilize your strengths to become the person you want to be.
4. Changing habits: It is time to quit smoking, lose weight, stop procrastinating, and get rid of old, unwanted habits.
5. Improving your relationships: You can be the partner, the friend, the parent, the employee, the boss, the person you want to be.

6. Changing your approach to life: How to adopt the right mindset and attitude, build self-esteem, and be confident.
7. Taking responsibility for everything that happens to you: Assume responsibility and understand that it is your choice how to respond to even the worst-case scenario.
8. Finding your purpose in life: How to create your mission and vision statement and be purpose-oriented.
9. Replacing negative thoughts with positive ones: It is time to reprogram your unconscious mind so you can finally get where you want to be.
10. Learning how to focus on what's important: See, appreciate, and instill all the beauty around you.
11. Finding motivation: The time has come to get inspired with the right motivation strategies.

<u>Coaching versus therapy</u>

Therapy is for people who suffer from a diagnosed mental disorder and it is usually focused on the past and traumas. Therapy is about mental health and is usually focused on the past while coaching is about mental growth and is usually focused on the future.

<u>Coaching versus counseling</u>

Counseling is a bit like coaching regarding the listening and the understanding part, but it is about giving advice to the person who is not happy with their life. Coaching, on the other hand, is about learning to advise yourself. Counseling is usually focused on the past while coaching is usually focused on the future.

Coaching versus mentoring

Mentoring is a bit like counseling but mostly focused on professional instead of personal goals. The mentor is considered to be an expert in their field and the mentee wants advice and solutions in the mentor's expertise field. Coaching, on the other hand, helps you understand yourself and identify what you want and how you will get it.

8.2.1 Life Coaching

Life coaching is about uncovering what you want and how you can get it, and about preparing you for success while you work on your vision statement. Life coaching helps you to explore your goals and dreams in your personal life and then unlocks your potential so you can get the desired results through a compass showing you the right direction.

Many people turn to friends and family for help and guidance when an issue occurs. The only difference between this type of life coaching and professional life coaching is the objectivity from the life coach's side. However, both types help you identify the underlying causes of your problems along with the solutions and empower you by helping you meet and exceed your goals and fill you up with confidence.

You may be stuck in a rut where you no longer experience joy and happiness. You may sometimes find facing the problem too hard. Everyone needs support, empowerment, and guidance at times. This is the way to examine other perspectives and reach your goals while you slowly gain confidence and focus on the future instead of analyzing the past.

The most important thing is that you can reach your potential through understanding and loving who you really are. This way, you will adopt a positive mindset and you will clarify what you want from life and how to get it. You will eventually find your peace by increasing your awareness on how your beliefs affect your life and which ones no longer serve you.

Life coaching is divided into relationship, marriage and, family coaching.

8.2.1.1 Relationship, Marriage, and Family

Good relationships make us happy. The qualities of a good relationship are the ability to communicate effectively, peaceful conflict resolution, and creation of a sense of belonging. Disagreeing from time to time is part of all relationships. However, the way people disagree is what may cause issues. Disagreements on serious matters beg for mutually satisfactory solutions and when this solution is hard to find, relationship coaching can help. The fact that you struggle with issues like this does not mean you need medical intervention. You just need an objective analysis of the current events and facilitation of a development plan that will help you achieve your goals.

Sometimes, our relationships lead us nowhere. There may be anger, resentment, disappointment, frustration, and a lot of other negative emotions piled up. What you need to understand is that there is no boredom in a romantic relationship. There is a negative emotion but definitely not boredom and you need to identify this underlying negative emotion.

When there are problems in our relationship, we can either ignore them by hiding them under the rug, we can self-improve by reading and attending workshops, or we can get help through coaching. Relationship coaching will help you heal your relationship or bring back the passion and fun a lot faster. You will set your goals and coaching will equip you with communication skills and conflict resolution strategies.

The important factor here is that you will understand how to address the challenges you face and how you can express yourself in a healthy way. You can learn how to effectively listen to your partner (or any other person you relate to) and understand them, you will be able to resolve your conflicts harmoniously and you will be strong enough to set healthy boundaries.

Relationship coaching helps if you are single, because you learn how to make better dating decisions, achieve happiness through true love, gain confidence, and get over an ex who has been hurting you. It also helps if you want to end your current relationship but do not know how to, or if you want to end and get over an abusive relationship. Remember that you need to be liberated from past hurt before you move on to a fresh start with a new person.

Through coaching, you ultimately become the best you can be and have the best relationship possible because you can understand your (potential) partner's views and why they behave the way they do. When you understand each other, you can choose to give up on limiting beliefs that no longer serve either of you, and finally you can make educated choices and adopt successful behaviors. This will result in bringing out the best in each other, or you may mutually realize and agree that you are not compatible and break up without second-guessing and hard feelings.

Keep in mind that relationship or marriage coaching will not necessarily save your relationship or marriage. It saves your mental wellness though by confirming that you make the best choice either sticking to the relationship or leaving it with no doubts or fear. Sometimes, you may be with the wrong partner, but this is fine as long as you assume responsibility and choose that this no longer serves you in achieving happiness.

When a couple decides to work together for their relationship, they need to realize that hard work will be expected from both of them. Both will need to commit to themselves and to each other. They will work as a team with identified and shared relationship (or marriage) goals. This is particularly important because oftentimes couples know that something is wrong but they cannot identify it and thus address it. If they are not interested in working as a team, then nothing will not be able to save the relationship.

Remember that even if you are the only one interested in coaching, you will still see a huge improvement, because you will learn how to address challenges, problems, and pain and you will return to the relationship empowered, provided that you commit to be open-minded and explore new ideas and perspectives.

Family coaching includes every relative, such as parents, siblings, and extended family members, and its goal is to support families to come closer and focus on values, effective communication, peaceful conflict resolution, empowerment of every family member, and experiencing joy living together and achieving shared goals.

Family coaching is about understanding the current family dynamics and facilitating the establishment of practices to achieve positive changes, which will in turn create tolerance of every individual in the family and an environment of peace, tranquility, love, and happiness, as long as every family member is willing to work hard.

Sometimes, even great parents need support and guidance so employing family coaching is nothing to be embarrassed about. On the contrary, it is a sign of how much you love and care about your family, and how much you want to develop your skills and knowledge so that you can raise your kids as best as possible. Or maybe you want to prepare yourself before giving birth to your kid and meeting the baby for the first time and learn how to cope with everyday life as a new parent. Or you may need guidance as your kids grow up. Perhaps your kid needs more support or a different form of discipline in order to reach their potential. If your kid's behavior affects other areas of life such as their performance at school or your social life, learn how you can address these matters without anger, despair, or frustration. Living with teenagers can be particularly challenging and venting on your teenage kid will only push them further away and they may even threaten you with school dropout, among other things, because they cannot understand that you worry about them. All they want is to gain their independence and manage their stress and peer pressure. It is significant that you are able to understand each other's perspective because this creates an environment of love, respect, balance, and peace at home.

Things are not always nice and easy for a couple. One of the partners may cheat and even have an affair, or they may have a secret (or not secret) addiction. This can hurt the other partner tremendously because of the betrayal. Under these circumstances, some people choose to separate or divorce. Others, however, try to stick together, for their own reasons. If you want to find out the root cause of the betrayal, then you need to visit a therapist. However, if you do not want to focus on that or seek justice, but you want to find the way to recover, you should employ family coaching instead with only one goal in mind; to rebuild trust and heal the wound so you can look at the future in an optimistic manner.

Family coaching is also helpful if you choose to separate or divorce. You have acknowledged that the relationship no longer works but being single right now hurts a lot, especially if you communicate with your ex for the sake of your kids. Just like with the loss of a loved one, you need support and empowerment and this is absolutely fine, because you have to remain strong for the rest of your family. Learning how to manage negative emotions so you do not need to hide your true feelings is practicing self-care and nothing to feel ashamed of.

The role of family coaching is to promote continuous and trusted communication between family members. When your entire family realizes and accepts that some things need to change, you will come up with plans to affect every family member's life positively.

8.2.2 Business Coaching

Business coaching is about uncovering what you want and how you can get it and about preparing you for success. It is about exploring your goals and dreams in your work life and then unlocking your potential and get the desired results by guidance toward the right direction. It will equip you with tools, knowledge, and skills in order to develop yourself so you can become your best self and cultivate your talents. Your performance, flexibility, and creativity will be improved and you will be better prepared to remove obstacles. This, of course, means many more opportunities will arise for you and greater overall success at your workplace.

Business coaching creates the desired environment for the employees as it helps them become happier, more productive, and recognized. Ultimately it helps people grow and develop new skills, it clarifies expectations, it gives feedback and tangible results, and it promotes trust and respect through collaboration.

Business coaching is further divided into leadership and career coaching.

8.2.2.1 Leadership and Career

Based on research conducted by Brandon Hall in 2015, 71% of companies feel that their current leaders are unable to carry their organization in the future. From my personal experience, I have to admit that 71% seems low. Yes, you read that correctly. I have worked for both startups and multinational companies and I have seen Greek, German, American, Indian, Canadian, French, Chinese, and Australian leaders who completely lacked leadership skills and mainly focused on their vanity. I am no way implying that everyone was like this, but the vast majority could not inspire their team. They could inspire fear through bullying though.

Leadership coaching is for open-minded people who understand that there are areas they can improve in and that they are not yet their best version. It is for anyone, spanning from C-level executives, to line managers, self-employed, or business owners and it is always a custom-made and collaborative partnership between the coach and the coachee. Occasionally, you may hear or come across the term "executive coaching," which is basically the same thing, but executive coaching is specifically the coaching that C-level executives receive.

Leadership coaching can help you develop a more effective leadership style, improve your communication skills, find the balance between life and work, manage your time correctly, plan your career advancement, develop your staff to operate with maximum performance, learn how to resolve conflict peacefully, develop your skills and talents in order to reach your goals, and fill you up with confidence. It will also help you learn how to remove obstacles and limiting beliefs on your way to success, identify the goals you need to set in order to achieve success, and facilitate your action planning and executing. It will ultimately maximize your performance and your work life will be improved and everyone around you at the workplace will become happier and more productive.

On top of that, leadership coaching will empower you and increase your creativity and accountability in the workplace. You will set goals dealing with behavior, performance, change, purpose, crisis, and development, in a safe and confidential environment. You will start to address matters and increase your self-awareness regarding your strengths and weaknesses. Remember that it will take you outside your comfort zone, but it will be totally worth it, as you will explore new options.

Career coaching is about identifying career goals and developing the appropriate action plan in order to achieve said goals. It will help you define and achieve your professional goals whether you want to stay in your current work situation or switch career paths.

Career coaching will enable you to achieve success, because it will help you feel confidence to pursue advancement opportunities and reach your potential. Career coaching is not only for those looking for a new job or a promotion. Career coaching is for everyone who feels unhappy with their work condition, or who wants to improve themselves in a series of skills, such as leadership, public speaking, communication, personal branding, conflict resolution, decision making, time management, work and life balance, productivity, negotiating, entrepreneurship, and more.

Through career coaching, you will learn more about yourself and current skills, goals, and ambitions so that you can later identify opportunities and learn how to remove obstacles and find the right job for you. You will focus on results, actions, and accountability, no matter whether you are unemployed, looking for a new job, are a fresh graduate looking for your first job, pursuing a promotion, or just wanting to switch career paths. The ultimate goal is that you feel confident about your future and have a more rewarding career with less or no stress.

Perhaps you are only interested in becoming more productive and a better communicator who will get along great with your colleagues, teams, and managers. Or you want to make sure you will not burn out. Or you want to help your kid select the right studies and future job according to their skills, aptitude, abilities, and interests. Career coaching is particularly helpful in all the aforementioned cases, as well as in case you want to start a new business, you want to retire but remain active in a workplace, or go back to work after a long hiatus.

I have personally changed profession several times so far, from translator to teacher, from recruiter to project manager, from leader to therapist and coach, and I know first-hand how important it is to feel empowered to change your career path. This is why it is very important to choose the right career coach for you.

Human resource executives may seem like a good idea if you look for a career coach but truth is that you should only work with a talent manager or a certified work performance assessor. Only then you will be able to receive guidance to improve your career progression, move into a new role, change career direction, find the balance between life and work by setting your priorities correctly, and overcome obstacles in the path to your fulfillment. It is rather helpful if your career coach is also, at least remotely, familiar with your own industry. You should ask this to make sure they understand the specific challenges in your current or desired industry.

Your career coach will provide you with insights, will help you address challenges that you have identified, and guide you to your path to success. You will also be able to collaborate with them on interviewing strategies and mock interviews, on the improvement of your digital profile and resume, on salary negotiation skills, on career and opportunities identification, on the creation of your personal brand, on the elimination of stage fright, on your prioritization, and on your career goal setting, planning, and executing. They will eliminate your limiting beliefs and will help you bring out your best self by equipping you with tools to solve conflicts and doubts regarding your career. You will gain confidence by identifying and maximizing your strengths while minimizing your weaknesses.

You spend at least one third of your life at work and you deserve to feel happy at work. A career coach will help you achieve happiness. Even if you currently have a good job, the career coach will help you set a goal for your future and work on your job satisfaction in five or ten years from now.

Before you reach out to a career coach, remember that they will not tell you what to do. They will help you discover what you want and how to achieve it. They will guide you but you will be accountable for your career decisions. You will learn from their tips but in order to see results, you have to work hard. You may practice mock interviews, but the coach will not update your resume or pitch for you. You will have to roll up your sleeves and be open to challenges because your coach will question your goals to make sure they are what you really want.

8.2.3 Why a Coach?

You may be wondering why you need a coach. The right coach helps you learn and bring out your best version so you can fill up with positivity and confidence. They will also help you navigate through challenges and obstacles. The truth is that some people can get there alone, and you may be able to do all of this on your own, without the help of a coach. The main difference is that you will need a lot more time on your own in comparison and that the coach will hold you accountable on your vision statement.

If you struggle with distractions or procrastination or a million other things, your coach will help you focus on what is important and increase your self-awareness. They will empower you to face your choices and understand that fear is normal and you just have to learn from it. They will also help you understand the role of your prioritization in your life. Your coach will ultimately help you understand the beliefs you have and how these affect every aspect of your life. This is why coaching is transformational. Because it can transform your life once you identify core issues that cause unhappiness or dissatisfaction, and it is up to you whether to move toward your goals or in the opposite direction.

Your coach will, metaphorically speaking, hold your hand and lead you to unknown territory and help you take the leap and assure you that the net will appear. The time to make your dreams come true has come and your coach will free you from limiting beliefs.

Remember that relationship dynamics have changed dramatically over the last 50 years. Both men and women in the Western world work, make their own money, prioritize their careers, make their own decisions, and live independently without having to explain their decisions or actions to anyone. Women haven't always had equal rights to men and were not expected to do all these things that are considered completely normal today, such as live independently and on their own.

Today, we realize that we want to feel love and a sense of belonging but without giving up on our freedom and personal space. So what are we supposed to do? Here comes the relationship coach, for example, to make you realize, among other things, that happiness and unhappiness derive from your relationship with yourself and not from your relationship with others.

The business world has also changed. Studies have shown that leadership coaching helps you reduce procrastination and facilitates goal achievement while it enhances performance. It also helps you to learn how to make the right choices and take educated decisions quickly or under pressure, as well as how to think freely and outside the box.

You can identify your strengths and understand why you do what you do and how your actions or inactions affect others. This, along with the elimination of limiting beliefs, empowers you by increasing your self-esteem and confidence. It also helps you deal with conflict more effectively and improve your communication so that you can express what you have in mind as well as receive clear messages and understand the sender's ideas. Finally, it assists in goal setting and respective action planning in order to achieve said goals.

Your coach will not and should not be a passive listener. They will help you find out who you really are, who you want to be, what you want to achieve, and how you can achieve it. They will help you set goals and remain focused on them, find alternative perspectives, prioritize based on your values, find your motivation, and finally develop and then execute an action plan in order to achieve your goals.

You will meet your coach on a regular basis. Your coach should be available through email during your entire coaching program and they should encourage you, motivate you, and celebrate with you every victory, no matter how small it may be. Remember that nowadays it is always easier to meet your coach online as it saves you both time and money.

The first coaching session is usually about matching and the coach asks you questions and makes notes about you and your life. You will tell them which areas you want to improve and you will agree on goals that will be broken down to more manageable objectives over the course of your next sessions.

The sessions where you meet with your coach are about setting the strategy that you will follow during the time between sessions. This means that it is up to you to follow the strategy you learnt and agreed with your coach. You need to focus and commit to your goal, because most of the work is done between these sessions when you apply your new skills and knowledge. If you face challenges, you can communicate with your coach or let them know next time you meet them but remember that it is you who drives the change.

The most successful people work with a coach because coaching works miracles. Coaching is based on the Socratic method, which is a form of cooperative argumentative dialogue, based on asking and answering questions that stimulate critical thinking and help the extraction of new ideas. Your coach helps you get where you want to be and trusts that you will do your own part because they know that you leave every session with a clear action plan.

Remember that your coach will collaborate with you and will remain focused on results and solutions while they will cultivate self-awareness and accountability, and facilitate your learning, development, and change.

Professional coaches have learnt to see the beauty and power in everyone and they are able to identify everyone's defense mechanisms and life strategies. At the end of the day, this is what coaching will help you do as well. Some people claim that the coach does not need to be an expert in their coachee's fields of work. This is not accurate and I would like to draw your attention to this matter, because unfortunately there are coaches out there who have neither the knowledge or the experience required to help you.

If you choose to work with a professional, please bear in mind that the success or failure of the coaching partly depends on finding the right coach for you. In order to choose the right coach for you, you need to consider a variety of things. So, make sure your coach is appropriately trained, ideally familiar with your work field, and make sure you match with them. It is of paramount importance that you and your coach click and they inspire you to trust them.

Something that my coachees keep telling me is that I somehow make them tell me things they have never confided before. It is extremely important that you feel the same way with your coach. You should also feel that they want to help you, they are objective, nonjudgmental, and they believe in you and your ability to reach your potential no matter how much you may resist this. Your coach needs to see the best in you and needs to want you to become the best version of yourself.

Coaching is not for everyone. It is certainly not for the faint of heart. Coaching is for those who are willing to discover their true self and transform their life. It is for the people who want to assume responsibility and think differently in order to fulfill their dreams. It is for those who are strong enough to admit they hold limiting beliefs and flawed internal representations that no longer serve them and will keep an open mind.

Keep in mind that coaching brings results when you discover the new strategy you need to follow through self-awareness. Remember that the focal point of coaching is about increasing your self-awareness. Therefore, in order to get the best out of coaching and become empowered, you need to invest and commit to both yourself and your coach. Commit that you want to become your best version, commit that you attend your sessions, and commit that you will stick to the new strategy and plan.

The work will be hard and you will need to be ready to make these beautiful changes in your life and you need to be ready to leave all your limiting beliefs behind. Now it is the time for you to rise so you need to be 100% determined that this is what you want.

Coaching is divided into life coaching and business coaching. These are further divided into relationship, marriage, and family coaching, and leadership and career coaching.

8.3 Self-Coaching

Now that you know how and why coaching can help you, you can start self-coaching. I believe in you and you are fully capable of starting the journey to your dreams and happiness through self-coaching.

You are able to coach yourself. It will just take longer to get to your desired results. Think of a small piece of IKEA furniture like a bedside table. You may build it on your own, without necessarily reading its manual, but would it not be a lot easier and faster if you read the manual that shows you the way?

In both cases, you may end up with a functional bedside table so you will have reached your goal. Unless you are a professional carpenter, chances are that if you had the manual as a guide, it would have been a lot easier and quicker.

Life and business coaches use a variety of tools, exercises, and techniques. In this section, you will find some exercises that you can use on your own and that can help you understand things about yourself, therefore increasing your self-awareness.

8.3.1 The Wheel of Life

The wheel of life always reminds me of the wheel of fortune and in a way they are similar. In both of them there are things you want. Unlike the wheel of fortune, luck is not required and you cannot bankrupt and lose your points with the wheel of life.

This is an effective tool for those who want to focus on their personal development and it is very easy to use in order to identify the aspects of your life that you are happy with and the aspects that you want to focus on in order to improve the quality of your life.

Look at each piece of the pie. If one or two pieces do not make sense to your current way of life, feel free to rename them or remove them completely. Now, think about the level of satisfaction with each one of them: Career, Finance, Personal Growth, Health, Family, Relationships, Social Life, Attitude.

Score each one by keeping in mind that 1 is the lowest level of satisfaction and 10 is the highest. Draw a line connecting all the segments of the pie. This is your overall life satisfaction at the moment. How does it relate to your desired life satisfaction? If it does not relate, try to identify at least one action to work on that will improve your score in one area of the wheel and which in turn will improve your total satisfaction level from life.

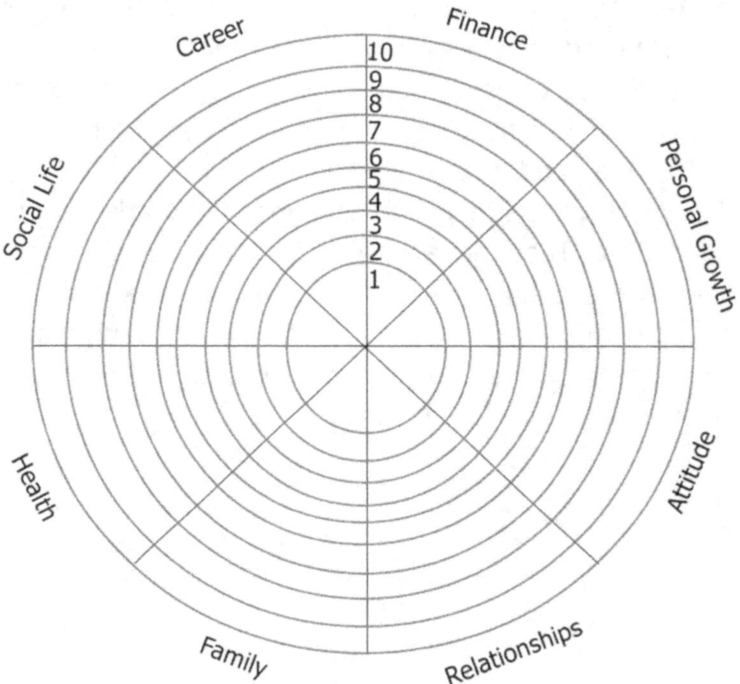

8.3.2 Spheres of Influence

We all share three distinct spheres of influence. These are things we can control, things we can influence, and things we cannot control or influence. You can use these three spheres of influence to clarify how things work on your end.

When we are upset or frustrated, we may think that everything is outside our control. However, this is not true. We always have one thing we can control and this is our attitude. If we think hard, we may find that there are actually more things we can control. If not, we may be able to influence some things in order to create a positive environment. We may not be able to control others, but we can influence them if we play by their rules.

For example, when I worked in Germany, an executive at my workplace used to bully everyone. However, if someone played along and just complimented him in order to empower his vanity, he could influence the executive's behavior, and they would have a good time serving him.

Finally, there are things that are indeed outside our control and influence. There are always factors that we cannot control or influence and this is part of life. We just need to accept it and stop wasting our energy in an effort of affecting them. We should conserve our energy and focus instead on the things that we can either control or influence.

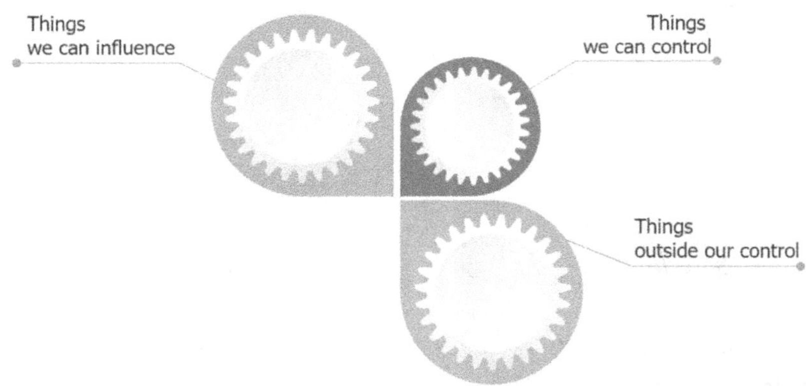

8.3.3 Keeping a Journal

Regular journaling helps you reflect on actions, inactions, and thoughts. Remember that this is your safe haven to express your thoughts and feelings and release negative emotions. Nobody will judge you. Once you write a few entries, start looking for patterns and observe common behaviors. When you observe how you think and feel, you will be able to understand

and learn more about yourself. You may also realize there are matters that need to be addressed.

You can update your journal every day or once a week. This is entirely up to you and how it makes you feel in the long run. Some people see that this habit makes them feel a lot better so they end up writing every day.

8.3.4 Three-Minute Meditation

You can do this every day before you get up and it will only take you a few minutes. Focus on your breathing for two minutes. Breathe deeply through your stomach, relax, quiet your mind, and remain still while you empty your mind. Then for the next minute, visualize who you want to be as a partner, friend, sibling, parent, employee, and so on. Imagine how it looks like to be this person. Get up and be the person you want to be.

8.3.5 The Gratitude Exercise

Expressing gratitude daily increases positive thinking and positive emotions. This is another easy exercise. When you lie down in bed to go to sleep, just think about three positive things that happened during your day or three things you feel grateful for, such as your relationship to another person, or the fact you are under a warm blanket.

8.3.6 Personal SWOT Analysis

You may have heard the term SWOT analysis at work. If not, SWOT stands for Strengths, Weaknesses, Opportunities, and Threats. It is easy to work on your personal SWOT analysis. Just create columns for each of these categories and list every one of your traits in the respective category.

This will help you learn even more about yourself and identify your strengths and weaknesses so that you know where to focus in order to improve areas of your life.

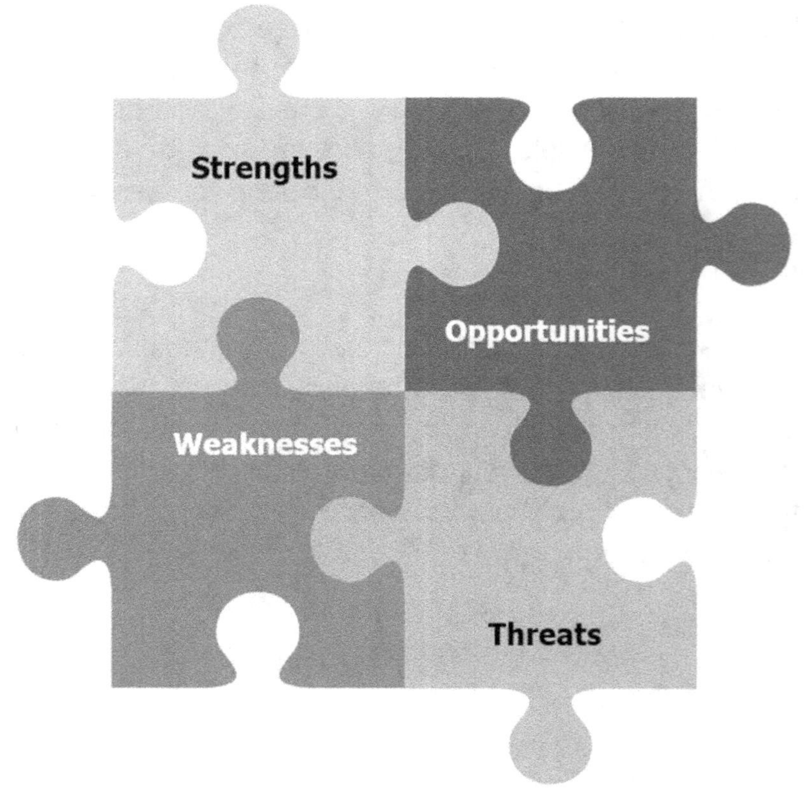

8.4 Conclusion

Now you know more about coaching; how it works, how it can help you, and what to expect from it. However, I cannot stress enough the importance of selecting the right coach in case you choose to work with a professional at some point of your life. There are many people out there calling themselves a coach but lack basic skills. You need to find someone that makes you feel safe, not because they shout when they speak publicly but because they have both a theoretical background and actual experience. The right coach is someone who inspires your trust.

Especially when it comes to business coaching, you need to invest in someone who will not only motivate you, guide you, and hold you accountable but also someone who could understand your position and even mentor you at times and teach you best practices. Only then the coach is able to ask you the right questions in the right timing and you can trust them.

Your coach needs to care about you as a person and not about your wallet. They will not try to eternalize your sessions so they can get money from you for years. They will not sell you false hope. They will genuinely be interested in getting to know you and your limiting beliefs, and help you to show compassion and professionalism. At the same time, they will encourage you to walk your path to success on your own and equip you with the tools to set and achieve your goals now and also in the future without assistance in the matters you have already addressed with your coach.

Your coach should celebrate with you and support you through hard times, they should work with you on your vision and help you focus on it when you get distracted, and they should facilitate your personal development and work toward your identified goals while they hold you accountable at all times. They will always explain to you things that you do not understand in a simple manner and they will collaborate with you to develop realistic plans with measurable results, always related to your goals, interests, and preferences. This is why a business coach experienced or knowledgeable in your field is crucial; so that you avoid costly experimenting with no results.

Several people are hesitant to ask for help or guidance. Assess your life. Have you reached your goals? Are you happy? If yes, this is fantastic! If not, why are you hesitant to move forward? This is the root cause why you have not reached success and happiness yet. You just need to be open-minded and ready to commit to the pathway of your freedom, success, and happiness.

Unfortunately, I have met people who prefer to live in misery and attention-seeking states. I have been volunteering in an online community to help anyone who claims to need help. I should mention that it is completely anonymous through private messaging, so privacy is never an issue. I have offered to help over 100 cases for free, because they claim they have no money. Only three of them were interested in actually getting help, and just one decided to work on their issues. You will see many people around you making excuses because they wish to remain in misery. I know you are not one of them, otherwise you would have never chosen this book. I know you want to excel and this is why I offered you my time, knowledge, and expertise writing this book with real strategies you can use at home. I believe in you. You just need to have a little faith in yourself and you will achieve your dreams.

8.5 Assignment for Reflection

Follow the instructions for the exercises of the Wheel of Life and the Spheres of Influence and see how happy you currently are in the various areas of your life and which factors you can influence, control, or do neither about.

9 Success Stories & Epilogue

9.1 Success Stories from Around the World

There are many famous people around the world who started with no help from anyone, and reached their goals. J.K. Rowling, the Harry Potter author who was famously rejected by publishers and Sigurd Wongraven who was rejected by music labels, and so many more.

However, there are so many inspiring stories by people who are not famous but are worth sharing. Just like the following stories.

9.1.1 Alex's Story

Alex, a half Greek-half German, has broken world records in different areas of skydiving as a wheelchair user, and also competes in International Bobsleigh Paralympic events. In 2009, he had a motorcycle accident that completely changed his life. However, he continued to pursue his life-long dream of becoming a skydiver. It took him four years of mental strength and resilience. Incredibly, he has jumped more than 100 times and is now inspiring others to break their own self-perceived and others' imposed limits! Alex inspires us to consider that if we really want something, then even the toughest obstacles can be overcome!

9.1.2 Dimitris' Story

Dimitris, a 38-year-old Greek man, was raised in a safe, risk-free environment. The school was near his home, and the square where he used to play with his friends was five minutes away. As a teenager, he was convinced that being a good student would probably secure his place at a good university and, this in turn, would secure him a good job. He would seldom leave his comfort zone and he was walking toward an almost predefined future. The environment (culture, family, education, social life, work) we live in formulates our personalities to a great extent. So, his formulated personality was, and still is to an extent, risk-averse, nurtured by the fear of failure and the unknown, which in turn, feeds anxiety and stress. When he was 24, he went through a stressful period, so he realized that he had to step up and challenge himself by starting anew. In 2009, he moved to the UK, where he still lives. He has a 4-year-old son, who is his biggest creation, and with his wife they strive for a beautiful family. He loves his job, because he has the opportunity to improve and develop people and processes along with himself. He has been shortlisted for the "National Emerging Business Improvement & Transformational Leader" award and for his company's Global Talent Scheme. His life purpose is to enjoy life as much as possible despite challenges, to be grateful for where he currently stands, and to be open for new adventures!

9.1.2 A Couple of Anonymous Stories

S.L. was a student of mine from the time I was a Project Management Diploma Assessor. She used to be a qualified accountant who would count beans, but she wanted a change. Nowadays, she is an Applied AI Researcher who counts cells applying her project management skills on international medical research projects. She claims that thanks to my guidance and attention to detail, I set a high standard for her because the tools and skills she learnt really help when leading projects. For most of her career, she was a treasury specialist until switching to an Artificial Intelligence (AI) Practitioner. She currently works in medical research on computer vision for pathology and has cofounded one of the most active, diverse, and inspiring AI communities of over 2,500 members to promote education in machine learning, and support their members in developing deep learning solutions. Faith has had a major role in sustaining her hope over her journey to her new career, and in 2019, her work was recognized and she was awarded the "Women in Technology, Western Australia, Tech [+] 20 Award!"

M.K. left her country five years ago to pursue her Master's degree in Marketing, in the Netherlands. After her studies, she started looking for a job. She applied to hundreds of jobs and went through several interviews, but she kept being rejected. She was disappointed and discouraged, so when a good friend told her about a sales position in the company she was working at, she applied immediately. She was not selected, but after five months they offered her a one-year contract for a similar position. She loved the environment and the people, and she made friends and a second family. But, a little over a year later, she started feeling miserable and anxious because her job wasn't fulfilling anymore. It had nothing to do with what she was looking for in her career. At the company, there was a small marketing team, and there were discussions about adding an extra position, so she expressed her interest immediately. Several colleagues and managers supported her, but it was a difficult decision that could only come from upper management. She had almost given up. She started developing her skills in several areas of marketing because she couldn't understand why she was still getting rejected by other companies. Then, one day, she was offered a transfer to the Marketing

Department, where she still happily works. The first months were difficult, because there were lots of expectations from everyone and herself and she wanted to bring something fresh and creative. She wanted to be the best and prove their choice was wise. She eventually did prove them right through hard work, persistence, and patience!

9.1.3 Natale Mastoroudes' Story

Back in early 2017, Natale Mastoroudes was an experienced Talent Acquisition Specialist, working for one of the largest B2B tech companies in the world, and ready for a new challenge. That's when her manager called her to discuss a new internal opportunity that had come up.

Natale was—and still is—based out of Cyprus. Her company had decided to make Cyprus, both the regional headquarters for its EMEA operations and a hub for new technologies. What this translated to was growth for the site, and they needed a Project Manager to ramp it up.

Timelines were impossible. The role required a familiarity with data analytics and project management skills that she didn't possess at the time. There was also a desperate need to grow the Talent Acquisition team both in numbers and skills in order to even stand a chance at meeting business needs. She wasn't confident she could pull it off, but she was willing to give it a shot.

For the next six months, she worked 70–80-hour weeks. It wasn't easy. She taught herself the required skills to get the job done. Her managers' support, mentoring, and assistance were key. They recruited and trained a talent acquisition team that worked like a well-oiled machine. Within just over a year, the site had doubled—from 350 employees to over 700. For her, the role was a career-changer. She is where she is today because she learned to stretch and grow as needed to get the job done, to say "yes" and then figure out the "how." And that's a lesson and experience she will always carry with her!

9.1.4 Barbara Sike's Story

Barbara Sike, a Hungarian woman, has been working since she was 18, almost always in multiple jobs simultaneously, so she has a wide variety of experiences of being managed by "bosses." She experienced being underestimated, silenced, and put down, but showed patience because she was moving toward her long-term goal to eventually be able to study abroad.

She started studying in London at the age of 25 with an overflowing ambition to become the best at what she does, even though she wasn't quite sure what that would be. Driven by that ambition, she got involved in pretty much every student activity from sports through societies to paid work, and was lucky enough to take the lead on many projects. All this helped her land a great internship-turned-full-time-role straight out of university.

Two years later, Barbara realized that even though she loved her job, she had started to lose her drive because of bad bosses who didn't give her the freedom to be creative. Even though she is a solution-oriented person and loves to grow with each role, she constantly felt rejection and started questioning her abilities and skills she had worked so hard to gain.

So, in 2020, in the middle of the pandemic lockdown, she took a deep breath and decided to exit the circle of trying and failing to fit into a toxic work environment. With a daring move, she quit her 9–5 job and started her freelance business. This gave her the opportunity to define herself as a professional and what makes her unique as a person so she started to regain her confidence. Two months later, she secured two major clients with a long-term contract, started publishing expert articles, and has learned more new skills. She has never felt more confident about a career decision!

9.1.5 Olgica Strezoska's Story

Two years ago, Olgica Strezoska worked at an IT company. The salary was good and the environment was great but she was completely unhappy, because she knew she could do more. She talked to management about her aspirations but they didn't see a position where she'd be a good fit.

Back then, she wanted to attend a Scrum course and asked the company if they would pay for her training. The company's response was that training was not suitable for her position. She was devastated but at the same time she was determined to do a career switch and take things into her own hands.

Olgica is a firm believer that if we want to improve, we must learn and challenge ourselves to step out of our comfort zone so she enrolled in a training program for Software Product Management and immediately realized that she wanted to become a Software Product Manager. She started studying hard for relevant certifications and, within two months, she became a certified Professional Scrum Master and Professional Scrum Product Owner. In the meantime, she was applying to all IT companies and got countless rejections because she lacked experience. She didn't give up. She believed in herself and she knew someone would eventually recognize her potential. And this is what happened.

She got a chance to work as a Product Owner and it was like her dream almost coming true. Unfortunately, not all her new colleagues were as supportive as Olgica hoped for, and this discouraged her in the beginning. Over that period, she got pregnant, but had a miscarriage during the first trimester. She only took one day off to rest and continued working even harder. As they say, it's not circumstances that shape you, it's how you respond to them. Life wasn't easy on her but it reminded her how strong she was. She didn't give up. She continued working on improving her skills. In the meantime, she felt the need to help people in the same position so she contacted an educational company and they accepted her Scrum training course. A few weeks later, she became a Scrum trainer and she was above the moon because she could help people that were eager to learn more or wanted to switch career paths.

Nowadays, after overcoming all obstacles, she works for one of the best companies in Macedonia as a Product Owner and has the ownership of four products. She is recognized, rewarded, and she feels she is at the right place because she loves every minute spent at work.

9.1.5 Elodie Rousset's Story

Elodie Rousset was born to an Afro-Asian French family. Her 18-year-old unmarried mother struggled to raise her and put her up for adoption when she was 4 years old. Elodie was in foster care for a year until she was adopted by a white French family in Southern France who were looking for an older child. From that early experience, Elodie realised that anyone can dream big and she feels grateful for the allies who supported her.

Being raised in a predominantly white environment in the 1990s and through university was a double-edged sword, from struggling to fully connect with people of her ethnicity to missing out on the best work opportunities for being the face of a minority group. Elodie pursued her career in London and she found balance in companies that celebrate diversity and alongside leaders who see people as individuals. Despite a turbulent early life, Elodie has always had a thirst for learning and believes that no one can take your knowledge away from you.

Elodie speaks four languages, she studied in France, Spain, and England, and with her Master's in Conference Interpreting, she landed interpreting internships at the EU and the UN. Her passion for computing started when she was introduced to programming at her primary school, so after 10 years of working in software translation management and interpreting assignments, she founded her own language consultancy that allowed her to work for the biggest Silicon Valley and European retail technology companies.

9.1.6 Athanasios' Story

Athanasios is a Greece-based man. His name means immortal in Greek. Truth is he defeated death. When he was 31 years old, he had a brain aneurysm rupture and he was in a coma for months. Doctors didn't know whether he could make it, let alone his condition when and if he woke up from the coma. They gave him less than 5% chance of survival.

The doctors said to his family "He's trying very hard." One day, two months later, they said "This is a neurological miracle. Not only has he survived but he has also won his quality of life." Athanasios woke up without suffering any neurological damage.

However, the second round of his battle had just begun. After three months of being in a coma, Athanasios had lost 66 pounds (30 kg) and his muscles were atrophied. The first few weeks, he couldn't even move his little finger. The first time he put his eyeglasses on, it was like he was lifting a heavyweight bar.

A few weeks later, he went home. Due to the Intensive Care Syndrome, his mind was confused and he developed anorexia. At 6ft 2", his weight was barely 108 pounds. Fortunately, that was good for his physical therapy. It took him almost an entire year of physical therapy to recover.

Nowadays, he is the owner of a software development company and he has reevaluated life and what is important. He appreciates everything he has in life and he is very close to his family and friends because all one needs is love.

9.2 Epilogue

What's the moral of the fairytale you read in the introduction of the book?

The king wanted to find a solution as quickly as possible. He did not care about the ramifications. He only wanted a solution. This is why he did not hear the guru's alternative solutions. We want to do everything quickly, not considering the consequences of our actions or inactions. We sometimes treat a threat or an obstacle as something more powerful than us, giving in to it. We let things waste us because it is faster, easier even, instead of facing them from afar and trying to eliminate them. Personal development, success, and happiness will not come overnight. We need to constantly aim at self-improvement and hard work. Even if we fail, we need to learn from our mistakes and be patient until we reach our goals.

We have all the answers inside us. All mentally healthy people can achieve every SMART goal they set because everyone can make it with the right guidance and support. This is why coaching is important. So that you can learn how to get these answers and move ahead on your own, without training wheels, to the path to your dreams.

Our DNA matters, and we do inherit traits from our parents and other ancestors. However, we should always keep in mind that our mindset and attitude also matter. These shape our responses and therefore experiences. As Dr. Judith S. Stern said "Genetics loads the gun and environment pulls the trigger."[25] I would paraphrase this as genetics and the environment load the gun, personality points the gun, and experience pulls the trigger.

Closing this book, I wholeheartedly hope that it reminded you how much you already have, it helped you, and taught you techniques about setting and achieving goals and drawing the map of your happiness. As a reminder, I would like to summarize the eight most important habits you need to adopt in order to be successful and happy.

1. **Be yourself**. Stop caring about what others think. Just be honest and tell the truth. Learn who you are and defend yourself consciously. Show everyone your real self so they can appreciate and/or like you for who you really are. Nobody is perfect so if you pretend something you are not, someone will sooner or later notice it. When you remain true to yourself, you are able to set clear and healthy boundaries that promote your physical and mental health. You need to assume responsibility only for your own actions and feelings.

2. **Be a great communicator**. Always communicate openly and make sure everyone understands what you want to convey whether it is a work briefing or your deepest dreams,

concerns, and needs. Remember to be a good listener as well. Pay attention to the person talking to you and show self-control and remain calm, no matter what the other person tells you. If you need a break, take it. Remember that asking for help is a sign of strength and not a sign of weakness. You acknowledge that you do not have everything in order to complete something successfully and you are confident enough to get all the required tools and information.

3. **Build trust**. Build relationships based on trust. Talk about your likes and dislikes, your worries, and accomplishments. Be there when someone needs you and encourage them. Show compassion, kindness, and respect, and accept people as they are. Do not try to change them, and appreciate them for who they are.

4. **Be positive**. Keep your positive attitude no matter how stressful or bad a day can be. Lift people up, laugh at their jokes, respect them, be kind to them with no expectations. Do not judge or hurt them. If you are wrong, apologize and show you mean it. Celebrate each other's victories! Share your knowledge, learn from others. Always focus on people's positive qualities and appreciate them for who they are and what they offer you emotionally when they are in your life. Remember to laugh and play! Laughter and playing keeps the small child we have inside us alive and this makes us look and feel younger!

5. **Be reliable**. Keep your word, show respect, and assume responsibility. Admit it if you are wrong. We all make mistakes, it is not a big deal but make sure that you keep your self-control, and you take actions to fix them. Do not compromise if something is against your values and beliefs, because it will backfire.

6. **Be solution-oriented**. Become one with your team, whether it is at work, friendships, or relationships. Do not compete against each other. Solve problems together when you identify them and encourage each other. Stand together against challenges and have each other's back.

7. **Prioritize your significant other**. Express your love in words and actions. Spend time together. Always be available if your significant other needs you, and share more with them than with anyone else. Set long-term goals, use "we" and make them your best friend.

8. **Manage negative emotions with DAWN**.
   Distance yourself from the emotion by taking a break.
   Approach as if it is someone else's emotion.
   Work on an action plan to change things you can change.
   Nurse yourself by practicing self-care.

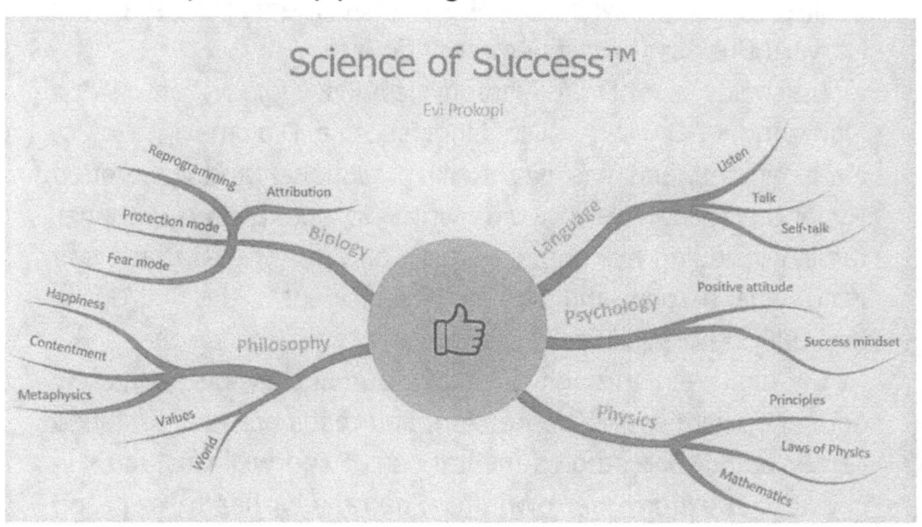

Author's Story

Dr. Evi Prokopi is a Success Coach, helping people achieve their personal and professional goals. She specializes in project human resource management and talent management, and she is a certified Work Performance Assessor and NLP Coach. She is a multicultural expert, having lived in six countries, traveled to 35 countries, and worked with people from 58 countries.

Evi was the first and youngest Greek female to ever speak at the Global Project Management Institute Congress in Spain, and she has also been a speaker at conferences in the UK and Greece. She has been invited to webinars, and currently works on Udemy courses. In 2020 she was the first Greek to make it to the list of the World's Top 100 HR Influencers, and she published an article about Responsible Leadership on the World Business Dialogue website while she became a member of the Harvard Business Review Advisory Council.

Evi holds a PhD in Metaphysical Psychology, an MA in Marketing, a BA in Applied Linguistics, a Diploma in Project Management, and she is a Reiki practitioner and a Certified Hypnotherapist. She loves to write, to spend time with her family (including her dog, Ragnar!), and in her spare time she is an aerial acrobat and acts as the President of the first Greek anti-bullying organization, Diexodos.

Evi has been through a lot of traumatic events ultimately ending up with severe depression, and that's how she switched career paths. She studied mental health and wellness and she chose to transform her own life. She now wishes to help and empower others to achieve their dreams and become happy.

1 Abraham H. Maslow (1954), "Hierarchy of Needs," *Motivation and Personality* (New York: Harper). [Image redrawn by E. Prokopi.]

2 S. Schachter and J. Singer (1962), "Cognitive, Social, and Physiological Determinants of Emotional State," *Psychological Review* 69(5):379–399.

3 Robert Ellsberg, Ed. (2001), *Thich Nhat Hanh: Essential Writings* (New York: Orbis Books), 37.

4 H. P. Blavatsky (1877), *Isis Unveiled: Secrets of the Ancient Wisdom Tradition* (Theosophical Publishing House).

5 W. D. Wattles (1910), *The Science of Getting Rich* (Holyoke, MA: E. Towne).

6 M. L. Kringelbach and K. C. Berridge (2010), "The Neuroscience of Happiness and Pleasure," *Soc. Res.* 77(2):659–678.

7 M. L. Kringelbach (2009), *The Pleasure Center: Trust Your Animal Instincts* (New York: Oxford University Press).

8 Strictly speaking they do, gravitationally, since they have mass, but the effect is ridiculously small.

9 Susannah Locke (4.16.2014) "Nuclear fusion could be the perfect energy source — so why can't we make it work? *Vox*.

10 Carlo Rovelli (7.8.2013), "Free Will, Determinism, Quantum Theory and Statistical Fluctuations: A Physicist's Take," *The Edge*.

11 C. S. Soon et al. (May 2008), "Unconscious Determinants of Free Decisions in the Human Brain," *Natural Neuroscience* 5:543–545.

12 Michele Debczak (August 9, 2017), "How Many Dimensions Are There?" *Mental Floss*.

13 C. Gustafson (2017), "Bruce Lipton, PhD: The Jump from Cell Culture to Consciousness," *Integr Med (Encinitas)* 16(6):44–50.

14 Albert Mehrabian (1971), *Silent Messages* (Belmont, CA: Wadsworth).

15 *The Punisher* (2017), "Momento Mori," season 1, episode 13, dir. Steve Lightfoot.

16 Paul Ekman (1992), "An Argument for Basic Emotions," *Cognition and Emotion* 6(3–4):169–200.

17 Paul Ekman (1999), "Basic Emotions," in *Handbook of Cognition and Emotion* (Sussex, UK: John. Wiley & Sons, Ltd.), 45–60.

18 Sigmund Freud (1972), *Mourning and Melancholia* (originally published 1917 as *Trauer und Melancholie*).

19 J. L. Elkhorne (March 1967), "Edison—The Fabulous Drone," 73 *Magazine*, Vol. XLVI, No. 3: 52.

20 Carl Jung, *Letters Vol. 1. 1906–1950.*

21 R. Dilts, J. Grinder, J. Delozier, and R. Bandler (1980), Neuro-Linguistic Programming: Volume I: The Study of the Structure of Subjective Experience (Cupertino, CA: Meta Publications).

22 Make sure you state it as a question but with no question mark. Use a period instead. Practice it aloud so you can get the grasp of it.

23 Project Management Institute, *"What Is Project Management,"* www.pmi.org/learn-about-PMI/what-is-project-management.

24 Martin Luther King (2012), *A Gift of Love: Sermons from Strength to Love and Other Preachings* (Boston, MA: Beacon Press), 128.

25 Felix Bronner, Ed. (2005), *Nutritional and Clinical Management of Chronic Conditions and Diseases* (Boca Raton, FL: CRC Press), 43.